"People concerned with the religious right's attempt to restrict the rights implicit in our First Amendment will find much in this book to consider."
—American Booksellers Foundation for Free Expression

"...fascinating... makes great reading for anyone interested in Church history, or even the rise of Western thought."
—Factsheet Five

"In today's 'Moral Majority' climate, with the increasing influence of right-wing extremists, this book is a chilling reminder that the 'Christian' message has not been good for everyone." *—NAPRA ReVIEW*

"...an interesting counterbalance to the more devotional titles found in most religion collections." *—Library Journal*

"There is much in this book that does bear out the stigma of a dark side: the Crusades, the Inquisition, witch hunts, etc."
—Small Press

"Written for the lay reader, this controversial book is especially relevant today as the religious right is attempting to assert greater influence in American politics and society."
—The Freethought Observer

"...charts the many instances of religious brutality and overbearing domination on the part of Christian believers, providing a strong history on the racist and sexist legacy of Christianity." *—Reviewer's Bookwatch*

"Ms. Ellerbe has written nothing less than a shocking exposé of Christian history over its entire existence."
—New Moon Rising

The Dark Side
of
Christian History

The Dark Side
of
Christian History

Helen Ellerbe

MORNINGSTAR BOOKS

Library of Congress Catalogue Number: 95-60339

Publisher's Cataloging in Publication

Ellerbe, Helen.
The dark side of Christian history / by Helen Ellerbe.
p. cm.
Includes bibliographical references and index.
ISBN 0-9644873-4-9

1. Christianity–Early church, ca. 30-600. 2. Christianity–
Middle Ages, 600-1500. 3. Christianity–Modern period, 1500-.
4. Theology, Doctrinal. 5. Philosophy and religion. I. Title.

BR145.2.E55 1995   209
QBI95-20064

This book is dedicated to
freedom and human dignity.

Contents

Preface

In June of 1995 the *Chicago Tribune* reported that Pope John Paul II had urged the Roman Catholic Church to seize the "particularly propitious" occasion of the new millennium to recognize "the dark side of its history."[1] In a 1994 confidential letter to cardinals which was later leaked to the Italian press, he asked,

> *How can one remain silent about the many forms of violence perpetrated in the name of the faith—wars of religion, tribunals of the Inquisition and other forms of violations of the rights of persons?*[2]

Unfortunately, too many have remained silent. Several years ago I listened in amazement as an acquaintance spoke of how the Christian Church had embodied the best of Western civilization and how it had brought peace and understanding to the people it touched. He seemed entirely unaware of the Church's dark past. I decided to prepare a short presentation chronicling the dark side of Christian history—a presentation to help balance the perception that organized Christianity has historically lived up to its professed principles and ideals.

I assumed that I would easily find all the information necessary for this presentation at the bookstore, but was soon shocked to find so little available on the subject. While historians have certainly written about the dark side of Christian history, their words have largely stayed within the confines of academe. And few have written of Christianity's role in creating a world in which people feel alienated from the sacred. Why, at a time when so many are searching for deeper spiritual meaning, isn't there more accessible information about the history of the institutions which are purported to convey such spiritual truth? Without understanding the dark side of religious history, one might think that religion and spirituality are one and the same. Yet, organized religion has a very long history of curtailing and containing spirituality, one's personal and private relationship with God, the sacred, or the divine.

This book is what became of that short presentation. My intention is to offer, not a complete picture of Christian history, but only the *side* which hurt so many and did such damage to spirituality. It is in no way intended to diminish the beautiful work that countless Christian men and women have done to truly help others. And it is certainly not intended as a defense of or tribute to any other religion.

Helen Ellerbe
February 1996

Introduction

The Christian church has left a legacy, a world view, that permeates every aspect of Western society, both secular and religious. It is a legacy that fosters sexism, racism, the intolerance of difference, and the desecration of the natural environment. The Church, throughout much of its history, has demonstrated a disregard for human freedom, dignity, and self-determination. It has attempted to control, contain and confine spirituality, the relationship between an individual and God. As a result, Christianity has helped to create a society in which people are alienated not only from each other but also from the divine.

This Christianity—called "orthodox Christianity" here—is embedded in the belief in a singular, solely masculine, authoritarian God who demands unquestioning obedience and who mercilessly punishes dissent. Orthodox Christians believe that fear is essential to sustain what they perceive to be a divinely ordained hierarchical order in which a celestial God reigns singularly at a pinnacle, far removed from the earth and all humankind.

While orthodox Christianity originally represented but one of many sets of early Christian beliefs, it was these Christians who came to wield political power. By adapting their Christianity to appeal to the Roman government, they won unprecedented authority and privilege. Their church became known as *the* Church. This newly acquired power enabled them to enforce conformity to their practices. Persecuting those who did not conform, however, required the Church to clarify its own doctrine and ideology, to define exactly what was and was not heresy. In doing so, the Church consistently chose tenets and ideologies that best supported its control over the individual and society.

As it took over leadership in Europe and the Roman Empire collapsed, the Church all but wiped out education, technology, science, medicine, history, art and commerce. The Church amassed enormous wealth as the rest of society languished in the dark ages. When dramatic social changes after the turn of the millennium brought an end to the isolation of the era, the Church fought to maintain its supremacy and control. It rallied an increasingly dissident society against perceived enemies, instigating attacks upon Muslims, Eastern Orthodox Christians, and Jews. When these crusades failed to subdue dissent, the Church turned its force against European society itself, launching a brutal assault upon southern France and instituting the Inquisition.

The crusades and even the early centuries of the Inquisition did little to teach people a true understanding of orthodox Christianity. It was the Protestant Reformation and the Catholic Counter Reformation that accomplished this. Only during the Reformation did the populace of Europe adopt more than a veneer of Christianity. The Reformation terrified people with threats of the devil and witchcraft. The common perception that the physical world was imbued with God's presence and with magic was replaced during the Reformation with a new belief that divine assistance was no longer possible and that the physical world belonged only to the devil. It was a three hundred year holocaust against all who dared believe in divine assistance and magic that finally secured the conversion of Europe to orthodox Christianity.

By convincing people that God was separate from the physical world, orthodox Christianity—perhaps unwittingly—laid the foundation for the modern world, a world believed to be mechanical and determined, a world in which God is at most a remote and impersonal creator. People came to attribute their sense of powerlessness, not so much to their sinful human nature as to their insignificance in such a world. The theories of scientists and philosophers such as Isaac Newton, René Descartes and Charles Darwin reinforced orthodox Christian beliefs such as the inevitability of struggle and the necessity for domination. Such beliefs, however, are now proving not only to have serious drawbacks, but also to be scientifically limited.

Orthodox Christianity has also had devastating impact upon humanity's relationship with nature. As people began to believe that God was removed from and disdainful of the physical world, they lost their reverence for nature. Holidays, which had helped people integrate the seasons with their lives, were changed into solemn commemorations of biblical events bearing no connection to the earth's cycles. The perception of time changed so that it no longer seemed related to seasonal cycles. Newtonian science seemed to confirm that the earth was no more than the inevitable result of the mechanistic operation of inanimate components; it confirmed that the earth lacked sanctity.

The dark side of Christian history can help us understand the severing of our connection with the sacred. It can teach us of the most insidious and damaging slavery of all: the control of people through dictating and containing their spirituality. This ignored side of history can illuminate the ideas and beliefs which foster the denigration of human rights, the intolerance of difference, and the desecration of the natural environment. Once recognized, we can prevent such beliefs from ever wreaking such destruction again. When we understand how we have come to be separated from the divine, we can begin to heal not only the scars, but the very alienation itself.

ﺿ   ﺿ   ﺿ

Chapter One

Seeds of Tyranny

100 - 400 C.E.

Those who sought to control spirituality, to restrict personal relationships with God, gained prominence within the first centuries of the Christian era. Their beliefs formed the ideological foundation for much of the dark side of the Christian church's history. Committed to the belief in singular supremacy, these orthodox Christians thought that fear and submission to hierarchical authority were imperative. Not all Christians agreed. In fact, contrary to the conventional depiction of the first centuries of Christianity as a time of harmony and unity, early Christians disagreed about everything from the nature of God and the roles of men and women to the way one finds enlightenment.

Perhaps most pivotal to the group of Christians who would triumph—called "orthodox Christians" here*—was the belief in a singular supremacy, the belief that divinity is manifest in only one image. The belief in a singular God differed radically from the widespread belief that divinity could be manifest in a multiplicity of forms and images. As people believe that God can

---

* The use of the term "orthodox" in this book refers to the traditional ideology within most denominations of Christianity, not to any specific church or denomination.

have but one face, so they tend to believe that worth or godliness among humans can also have but one face. Different genders, races, classes, or beliefs are all ordered as better-than or less-than one another. Even the notion of two differing opinions existing harmoniously becomes foreign; one must prevail and be superior to the other.

Within such a belief structure, God is understood to reign singularly from the pinnacle of a hierarchy based not upon love and support, but upon fear. The Bible repeatedly exhorts people to fear God: "Fear God, and keep His commandments: for this is the whole duty of man."[1] "Blessed is everyone that feareth the Lord."[2] "Fear Him, which after He hath killed hath power to cast into hell; yea, I say unto you, Fear Him."[3] The third century Church Father, Tertullian, could not imagine how God could *not* demand fear:

> *But how are you going to love, without some fear that you do not love? Surely [such a God] is neither your Father, towards whom your love for duty's sake should be consistent with fear because of His power; nor your proper Lord, whom you should love for His humanity and fear as your teacher.*[4]

One's beliefs about God have impact upon one's beliefs about society. As the Lord's Prayer states, God's will should "be done on earth as it is in heaven." Orthodox Christians believed that people should fear their earthly ruler as they fear God. The fourth century St. John Chrysostom describes the absolute necessity for fear:

> *...if you were to deprive the world of magistrates and the fear that comes from them, houses, cities and nations would fall upon one another in unrestrained confusion, there being no one to repress, or repel, or persuade them to be peaceful through the fear of punishment.*[5]

To the orthodox, fear was essential to maintaining order.

Christians, such as the second century Marcion, who stressed the merciful, forgiving and loving nature of God, found themselves at odds with the orthodox. In orthodox Christian eyes, God must be prone to anger and demand discipline and punishment. Tertullian wrote:

> Now, if [Marcion's God] is susceptible of no feeling of rivalry, or anger, or damage, or injury, as one who refrains from exercising judicial power, I cannot tell how any system of discipline—and that, too, a plenary one—can be consistent in him.[6]

Scholars have suggested that the first line of the Christian creed, "I believe in one God, Father Almighty, Maker of heaven and earth," was originally written to exclude Marcion's followers by emphasizing the monotheistic and judgmental nature of God.[7]

Orthodox Christians placed great importance upon the singular authority of the bishop, upon rankings within the clergy, and upon distinction between the clergy and the laity. As there is only one God in heaven, declared the first century bishop, Ignatius of Antioch, so there can be only one bishop in the Church.[8] "Your bishop presides in the place of God, and your [priests] in the place... of the apostles," he wrote. "Apart from these, there is no church."[9] Such beliefs and attitudes, however, were certainly not shared by all Christians. The orthodox emphasized rank to such an extent that one Gnostic Christian wrote of them: "They wanted to command one another, outrivalling one another in their vain ambition," lusting "for power over one another," "each one imagining that he is superior to the others."[10]

Not all Christians accepted the belief in singular supremacy. Some Gnostic Christians understood God to be multi-faceted, having both masculine and feminine aspects. Some thought of the divine as a dyad; one side being "the Ineffable, the Depth, the

Primal Father" while the other side was "Grace, Silence, the Womb and Mother of the All."[11] In the Gnostic *Apocryphon of John*, a vision of God appears saying, "I am the Father, I am the Mother, I am the Child."[12] Theodotus, a Gnostic teacher, said, "each one knows the Lord after his own fashion, and not all in the same way."[13] To root out Gnostic Christians from the orthodox, the second century orthodox Bishop Irenaeus encouraged Christians to "confess with the tongue one God the Father."[14]

Without the belief in singular supremacy, it followed that Gnostic Christians would also reject hierarchical order and strict rankings within their church. In contrast to the orthodox Ignatius of Antioch who believed that the rankings of bishop, priest and deacon mirrored the heavenly hierarchy,[15] some Gnostic Christians did not even differentiate between clergy and laity, much less between stations of the clergy. Tertullian described the Gnostics:

> So today one man is bishop and tomorrow another; the person who is a deacon today, tomorrow is a reader; the one who is a priest today is a layman tomorrow; for even on the laity they impose the functions of priesthood![16]

And:

> ...they all have access equally, they listen equally, they pray equally—even pagans, if any happen to come... They also share the kiss of peace with all who come...[17]

Within an orthodox belief structure, there is no understanding of shared authority and supremacy between genders; one must be superior to the other. Perceiving the singular face of God to be male, orthodox Christians considered male supremacy an extension of heavenly order. St. Augustine wrote in the early fifth century, "we must conclude, that a husband is meant to rule over his wife as the spirit rules over the flesh."[18] In his first letter to the Corinthians, St. Paul tried to explain the reason for male supremacy:

> *For a man did not originally spring from woman, but woman was made out of man; and was not created for woman's sake, but woman for the sake of man.*[19]

As late as 1977, Pope Paul VI still explained that women were barred from the priesthood "because our Lord was a man."[20]

Among the orthodox, women were to take submissive roles. In the first letter to Timothy, St. Paul says:

> *Let a woman learn in silence with all submissiveness, I permit no woman to teach or to have authority over men; she is to keep silent.*[21]

When Christian monks in the fourth century hacked the great scholar Hypatia to death with oyster shells, St. Cyril explained that it was because she was an iniquitous female who had presumed, against God's commandments, to teach men.[22]

There were early Christians, however, who embraced neither the idea that God is exclusively male, nor the concept of male supremacy. An early group known as the Essenes, many of whose writings have been discovered in the Dead Sea Scrolls, thought of divinity as having a feminine aspect. In the Essene *Gospel of Peace*, Jesus says, "I will lead you into the kingdom of our Mother's angels..."[23] A Gnostic text tells how Eve, the daughter of Sophia who had wished the first heavenly light into the world, gives life to Adam:

> *...[Eve] said, 'Adam, live! Rise up on the earth!' Immediately her word became a deed. For when Adam rose up, immediately he opened his eyes. When he saw her, he said, 'You will be called "the mother of the living" because you are the one who gave me life.'*[24]

Not all early Christian women accepted subservient roles.

While Gnostics held a wide range of views, several of their writings refer to Mary Magdalene as one of the most important leaders of the early Christian movement. Some believed that she was the first to see Jesus Christ resurrected and that she challenged Peter's authority as part of the emerging Church hierarchy. Tertullian was appalled at the role of women among Gnostics:

> The... women of the heretics, how wanton they
> are! For they are bold enough to teach, to
> dispute, to enact exorcisms, to undertake cures
> —it may be even to baptize![25]

Another point of contention among Christians dealt with the nature of truth and how an individual might become enlightened. Much of this argument centered around the resurrection of Christ, around whether it was Christ's physical body or his spirit that had been resurrected. Orthodox Christians insisted that it had been Christ's physical body, to use Tertullian's words, his "flesh suffused with blood, built up with bones, interwoven with nerves, entwined with veins..."[26] They believed that since it was Christ's physical body, the resurrection was a one-time occurrence, never to be experienced again.

The orthodox insisted that one could learn of Christ only through those who had experienced this resurrection, the Apostles, or those men appointed as their successors. This confined power and authority to a small few and established a specific chain of command.[27] It restricted the avenues through which one could discover God. Orthodox, catholic ("universal") Christians claimed to be those appointed successors of the Apostles and thus the only ones who could enlighten others. Bishop Irenaeus declared:

> It is incumbent to obey the priests who are in the
> Church... those who possess the succession from
> the apostles; those who, together with the

succession of the episcopate, have received the
certain gift of truth.[28]

To this day the Pope traces his authority and primacy to Peter himself, "first of the apostles," since he was "first witness of the resurrection."[29]

Some Gnostics, however, called the belief in the resurrection of Christ's literal, physical body rather than his spirit the "faith of fools."[30] They took issue both with the idea that anyone had seen Christ in physical body after the resurrection as well as with the assertion that Peter had been the first to experience the resurrected Christ. Even the canonized gospels of Mark and John relate how Jesus first appeared, not to Peter or to the Apostles, but to Mary Magdalene.[31] By Jesus's saying to Mary "Touch me not,"[32] some think that Jesus implied he was in spirit form rather than in physical body. Believing Christ's spirit to have been resurrected suggests that anyone, regardless of his or her rank, could experience or "see the Lord" in dreams or visions. Anyone could become empowered with the same authority as the Apostles.[33] Anyone could have access to and develop his or her own relationship with God.

Christians disagreed about the very nature of truth. To the orthodox, who believed that truth could come only through the successors of the Apostles, truth was static and never-changing. It had been revealed only once at the resurrection. Consequently, they thought that one should learn of God only through the Church, not from personal inquiry and not from one's own experience. Blind faith was considered more important than personal understanding. Bishop Irenaeus cautioned not to seek answers "such as every one discovers for himself," but rather to accept in faith that which the Church teaches and which "can be clearly, unambiguously and harmoniously understood by all."[34] He wrote, "If... we cannot discover explanations of all those things in Scripture... we should leave things of that nature to God who created us, being most properly assured that the

Scriptures are indeed perfect."[35] Tertullian declared:

> *We want no curious disputation after possessing Christ Jesus, no inquisition after enjoying the gospel! With our faith, we desire no further belief.*[36]

One should unquestioningly accept and submit to whatever the Church teaches.

Indeed, orthodox Christians deemed rigorous personal pursuit of truth and understanding an indication of heresy. As Tertullian wrote:

> *This rule... was taught by Christ, and raises amongst ourselves no other questions than those which heresies introduce, and which make men heretics.*[37]

And:

> *But on what ground are heretics strangers and enemies to the apostles, if it be not from the difference of their teaching, which each individual of his own mere will has either advanced or received?*[38]

Since the orthodox believed truth to be known only to the successors of the Apostles, one could learn of it only by accepting the Church's teachings in blind faith.

Others, however, believing that Christ's spirit and presence could be experienced by anyone at any time, considered truth to be dynamic and ever-increasing. Some Gnostics believed that truth and *Gnosis* or "knowledge" was found, not by looking to the Church, but by looking within oneself. Self-knowledge would lead to knowing God. A Gnostic teacher named Monoimus wrote:

> *Look for (God) by taking yourself as the starting point... Learn the sources of sorrow, joy, love, hate... If you carefully investigate these matters you will find him in yourself.*[39]

The first century Simon Magus taught that within each human being dwells "the Boundless power, which... is the root of the universe."[40]   The path to enlightenment involved not simply accepting the words of the Church on faith, but an active personal search for understanding. A Gnostic text reads "...the rational soul who wearied herself in seeking—she learned about God."[41]

These Christians believed self-exploration to be imperative to one's spiritual path. In the Gnostic *Gospel According to Thomas*, Jesus says:

If you bring forth what is within you, what you
bring forth will save you. If you do not bring
forth what is within you, what you do not bring
forth will destroy you.[42]

They believed that searching could dispel the ignorance that produced a nightmarish existence in which one is caught in "many illusions" and experiences "terror and confusion and instability and doubt and division."[43] The *Gospel of Truth* reads:

ignorance... brought about anguish and terror.
And the anguish grew solid like a fog, so that no
one was able to see.[44]

Searching within oneself could bring the knowledge and enlightenment to dispel such ignorance. They believed that Jesus had encouraged self-exploration. Jesus said, "Seek, and ye shall find; knock, and it shall be opened unto you" and "the Kingdom of God is within you."[45]

Just as the orthodox wanted to control truth, so they wanted strict control over who could dispense that truth. Early Christians differed sharply about the role of the Church. Gnostic Christians who valued personal exploration believed that the structure of the Church should remain flexible, while orthodox Christians insisted upon strict adherence to a singular Church.[46] Bishop Irenaeus insisted there could be only one church, and outside that church "there is no salvation."[47] He said of the

Church, "she is the entrance to life, all others are thieves and robbers."[48] Ignatius, the Bishop of Antioch, wrote, "Let no man deceive himself: if any one be not within the altar, he is deprived of the bread of God."[49] And Clement, the Bishop of Rome from 90-100 C.E., argued that God alone rules all things, that He lays down the law, punishing rebels and rewarding the obedient, and that His authority is delegated to Church leaders. Clement went as far as to say that whoever disobeys these divinely ordained authorities has disobeyed God Himself and should receive the death penalty.[50]

Long before the Church's attempt to control spirituality would take its devastating toll, the seeds of its tyranny were evident in the ideology of early orthodox Christians. Their belief in singular supremacy limited the way one could understand God and it eliminated any representation of shared supremacy. It encouraged a fear-based authoritarian structure that segregates people into positions of superiority or inferiority, restricts personal empowerment, and demands unquestioning obedience. Although orthodox Christians represented only one of many early branches, within a few centuries they had effectively suppressed the diversity of early beliefs and ideas. Orthodox Christian beliefs became synonymous with Christianity itself.

≈ ≈ ≈

Chapter Two

Political Maneuvering: Making Christianity Palatable to the Romans

200 - 500 C.E.

Christianity owes its large membership to the political maneuvering of orthodox Christians. They succeeded in turning Christianity from an abhorred minor cult into the official religion of the Roman Empire. Their goal was to create what Bishop Irenaeus called "the catholic church dispersed throughout the whole world, even to the ends of the earth."[1] To that end, they used nearly any means. They revised Christian writings and adapted their principles to make Christianity more acceptable. They pandered to Roman authorities. They incorporated elements of paganism. Orthodox Christianity appealed to the government, not as a religion that would encourage enlightenment or spirituality, but rather as one that would bring order and conformity to the faltering empire. The Roman government in turn granted orthodox Christians unprecedented privilege, enabling the Christian church to become the very sort of authoritarian power that Jesus had resisted.

Winning acceptance for Christianity was no small feat; Christians were not well-liked within the Roman Empire.

Romans had easily incorporated new gods and goddesses into their pantheon with the hope of adding to their own protection and security. The 313 C.E. Edict of Milan, for example, granted everyone religious freedom so "whatever divinity (is) enthroned in heaven may be well-disposed and propitious towards us and all those under our authority."[2] Christians, however, believing theirs to be the one and only God, refused to allow Him to be worshipped alongside others. When they refused to profess loyalty to the Roman pantheon of gods, Christians were seen as likely traitors to the Roman state. For once Roman emperors began to represent themselves as divine, loyalty to the Roman gods also symbolized loyalty to the Roman state.

Christians held attitudes that did little to endear them to Romans. Bishop Irenaeus, for example, declared, "We have no need of the law for we are already far above it in our godly behavior."[3]   Accounts from around the year 200 reflect the dislike Romans had for Christians:

> ...they were 'the ultimate filth', a gang 'of ignorant men and credulous women', who 'with meetings at night, solemn fasts and inhuman food' made up 'a hole-in-the-corner, shadow-loving crew', 'silent in public but clacking away in corners', 'spitting on the gods and laughing at holy things...'[4]

Yet, despite such an environment, Christians won not only acceptance but political prominence as the official religion of the Roman Empire under Emperor Constantine in the fourth century.

The orthodox used politically expedient means to accomplish such ends. They designed an organization not to encourage spirituality, but to manage large numbers of people. They simplified the criteria for membership. The Catholic Church decided that anyone who confessed the Creed, accepted baptism, participated in worship, obeyed the Church hierarchy and believed "the one and only truth from the apostles, which is handed down by the Church"[5] was a Christian. As one historian writes, such criteria suggest that "to achieve salvation, an ignoramus need only believe without understanding and obey the authorities..."[6] The orthodox ignored the argument that a true Christian could only be identified by his or her behavior and maturity, not by simply going through the motions of ritual. Some Gnostic Christians, for example, insisted that Jesus had said, "By their fruits ye shall know them..."[7] Baptism did not necessarily make one a Christian, they said, since many people "go down into the water and come up without having received anything."[8] The simple standards of the orthodox, however, made it much easier to garner a large following.

Orthodox Christians assembled the Bible not to bring all the gospels together, but rather to encourage uniformity. From the plethora of Christian gospels, Bishop Irenaeus compiled the first list of biblical writings that resemble today's New Testament around 180 C.E. By 393 and 397, Bishop Athanasius had a similar list ratified by the Church councils of Hippo and Carthage.[9] By prohibiting and burning any other writings, the Catholic Church eventually gave the impression that this Bible and its four canonized Gospels represented the only original Christian view. And yet, as late as 450, Theodore of Cyrrhus said that there were at least 200 different gospels circulating in his own diocese.[10] Even the *Catholic Encyclopedia* now admits that the "idea of a complete and clear-cut canon of the New Testament existing from the beginning... has no foundation in history."[11]

Beyond choosing from the many gospels and writings to construct the Bible, the Church edited its message with each translation. The Roman philosopher Celsus, witness to the falsification of Christian writings already in the second century, said of the revisionists,

> *Some of them, as it were in a drunken state*
> *producing self-induced visions, remodel their*

Gospel from its first written form, and reform it
so that they may be able to refute the objections
brought against it.[12]

The *Catholic Encyclopedia* concedes that "In all the departments forgery and interpolation as well as ignorance had wrought mischief on a grand scale."[13] Despite Church prohibitions against any further research into the origins of the Gospels, scholars have shown that all four canonized Gospels have been doctored and revised.[14] While the Church claimed that truth was static in nature and had been revealed only once, it continually found cause for changing that truth.

Attempts at uniformity did not entirely succeed. Even the four canonized Gospels contradict one another. The Gospel of Matthew tells us that Jesus was an aristocrat descended from David via Solomon, whereas the Gospel of Luke tells us that Jesus was from much more humble stock, and the Gospel of Mark says that Jesus was born to a poor carpenter. At his birth, Jesus was visited by kings according to Matthew, but according to Luke, he was visited by shepherds. And at Jesus's death, the Gospels of Mark and Matthew tell us that Jesus's last words were "My God, my God, why hast thou forsaken me?" But according to Luke, he said, "Father, into thy hands I commend my spirit," and in John he says simply, "it is finished."[15] As the authors of *Holy Blood, Holy Grail* ask, "How can (the Gospels) be unimpugnable when they impugn each other?"[16]

Yet, it was the Church's insistence upon uniformity that appealed to the Roman Emperor Constantine. Constantine, a man who had his own son executed and his wife boiled alive,[17] saw in Christianity a pragmatic means of bolstering his own military power and uniting the vast and troubled Roman Empire. The story is told of Constantine's dream which led to his acceptance of Christianity in which he saw a cross in the sky inscribed with the words, "In this sign thou shalt conquer." While he personally converted to Christianity only on his deathbed, Constantine recognized Christianity as a means of conquering dissention within the Roman Empire and instated it as the Empire's official religion.

Orthodox Christians dissociated Christianity from political insurgence. In all likelihood, they compromised the truth of Jesus's political involvement, holding Jews rather than Romans accountable for his death. The canonized Gospels conspicuously ignore the tension of increasing Jewish resistance to the Roman occupation of Judea during Jesus's lifetime. One exception is in the Gospel of Luke when it recounts how authorities "found this man [Jesus] perverting our nation, and forbidding [Jews] to give tribute to Caesar."[18] Less than 40 years after Jesus's death, that tension erupted into a violent war between the Roman army and Jews.

Jesus was probably engaged in the concerns of his time as both a political and spiritual leader. The term *Christ*, both in Hebrew and in Greek, was a functional title for a king or a leader.[19] Given the political environment, it is far more likely that the Romans—not the Jews—killed him for his political activity. Crucifixion had been the standard Roman punishment for sedition and the cross a symbol of Jewish resistance to Roman occupation.[20] Blaming Jews for Jesus's death was most likely a convenient means of obscuring Jesus's political involvement and dissociating Christianity from political rebellion.[21]

Once Christianity gained prominence, the orthodox allowed the Roman emperor to directly influence Christian doctrine. To settle ideological disputes in the Church, Constantine introduced and presided over the first ecumenical council at Nicea in 325. In his book *The Heretics*, Walter Nigg describes the means of

---

2.1 The Roman Emperor Constantine believed Christianity would provide a means to greater political and military power. This illustration depicts him on the eve of an important battle when he is said to have seen a cross in the sky with the words, "In this sign thou shalt conquer."

reaching a consensus:

> *Constantine, who treated religious questions solely from a political point of view, assured unanimity by banishing all the bishops who would not sign the new profession of faith. In this way unity was achieved. 'It was altogether unheard-of that a universal creed should be instituted solely on the authority of the emperor, who as a catechumen was not even admitted to the mystery of the Eucharist and was totally unempowered to rule on the highest mysteries of the faith. Not a single bishop said a single word against this monstrous thing.'[22]*

One of the political decisions reached at the Council of Nicea established the Nicene creed, a means of keeping the belief in singular supremacy intact while simultaneously incorporating Jesus into the image of God. Jesus was not to be considered mortal; he was an aspect of God which could be understood as the Father, Son and Holy Ghost. This new Holy Trinity mimicked a much older portrait of divinity that embodied the value of difference. For instance, the vision of God in the Gnostic *Secret Book of John*, "I am the Father, I am the Mother, I am the Child,"[23] illustrates the concept of synergy where the whole created is greater than the sum of the parts. Another text called *The Sophia of Jesus Christ* tells how masculine and feminine energies together created a

> *...first-begotten, androgynous son. His male name is called 'First-Begettress Sophia, Mother*

2.2 A depiction of the Christian Trinity, a concept that allowed Jesus to be considered part of God while still maintaining the belief in a singular supremacy. It took the older concept of trinity illustrating the value of difference, in which a man and a woman together create a synergy, something that is greater than them both, and replaced it with a trinity that exalted sameness.

TRINITY.

of the Universe.' Some call her 'Love.' Now the first-begotten is called 'Christ.'[24]
Even the later Islamic Koran mistook the Christian Trinity for this archetypal one, referring to it as the trinity of God, Mary and Jesus.[25]

The Nicene Creed, however, established a trinity that extolled sameness and singularity. All reference to a synergy, an energy, a magic, that could result from two different people coming together was lost. The council eliminated the image of father, mother and child, replacing the Hebrew feminine term for spirit, *ruah*, with the Greek neuter term, *pneuma*.[26] The trinity was now comprised of the father, the son, and a neuter, sexless spirit. Christians depicted it as three young men of identical shape and appearance.[27] Later medieval sermons would compare the trinity "to identical reflections in the several fragments of a broken mirror or to the identical composition of water, snow and ice."[28] Two popes would ban the seventeenth century Spanish nun Maria d'Agreda's book, *The Mystical City of God*, for implying a trinity between God, Mary and Jesus.[29] All allusions to the value of difference were lost; divinity was to be perceived as a singular image, either male or neuter but never female.

Yet, it was their belief in the many faces of God that helped Romans accommodate Christianity, not the uniqueness of Christian theology. Christianity resembled certain elements of Roman belief, particularly the worship of Mithra, or Mithraism. As "Protector of the Empire,"[30] Mithra was closely tied to the sun gods, Helios and Apollo. Mithra's birthday on December 25, close to the winter solstice, became Jesus's birthday. Shepherds were to have witnessed Mithra's birth and were to have partaken in a last supper with Mithra before he returned to heaven.[31] Mithra's ascension, correlating to the sun's return to prominence

---

2.3 Holding Jews rather than Romans accountable for Jesus's crucifixion was most likely a means of making Christianity more acceptable to the Roman government by ignoring Jesus's probable role as a political rebel.

around the spring equinox, became the Christian holiday of Easter. Christians took over a cave-temple dedicated to Mithra in Rome on the Vatican Hill, making it the seat of the Catholic Church. The Mithraic high priest's title, *Pater Patrum*, soon became the title for the bishop of Rome, *Papa* or Pope.[32] The fathers of Christianity explained the remarkable similarities of Mithraism as the work of the devil, declaring the much older legends of Mithraism to be an insidious imitation of the one true faith.[33]

With no initial support from the Church, the figure of Mary became revered as an image for the feminine aspect of God. As Christianity paralleled Mithraism, so the worship of Mary resembled the worship of faces of the Goddess, particularly that of mother/son traditions such as Isis/Horus, Juno/Mars, Cybele/ Attis, and Neith/Ra. Mary was perceived to be a more accessible, approachable and humane figure than the judgmental, almighty God. She was more gentle and forgiving and much more likely to help one in everyday affairs. The fifth century historian Sozomen describes Mary's character in his writing of the Anastasia in Constantinople:

> *A divine power was there manifested, and was helpful both in waking visions and in dreams, often for the relief of many diseases and for those afflicted by some sudden transmutation in their affairs. The power was attributed to Mary, the Mother of God, the holy Virgin, for she does manifest herself in this way.*[34]

Neither the Bible nor the early Church encouraged Marian worship or even recognized Mary as a saint.[35] Although the Council of Nicea reaffirmed that Christ was indeed born from the Virgin Mary, the fourth century Bishop Epiphanius expressed

---

2.4 The early Church reluctantly permitted worship of the Virgin Mary. In doing so, it allowed pre-Christian veneration of feminine divinity to continue as Marian worship.

the sentiment of orthodox Christians: "Let the Father, the Son and the Holy Spirit be worshipped, but let no one worship Mary."[36] During the first five centuries, Christian art depicted Mary in a less venerable state than even the Magi, the three wise men, who wore halos while Mary wore none.[37] St. Chrysostom in the fourth century accused Mary of trying to domineer and "make herself illustrious through her son."[38] Diminishing Mary's significance was a way of discouraging her association with older pre-Christian faces of the Goddess. Bishop Epiphanius wrote:

> *God came down from heaven, the Word clothed himself in flesh from a holy Virgin, not, assuredly, that the Virgin should be adored, nor to make a goddess of her, nor that we should offer sacrifice in her name, nor that, now after so many generations, women should once again be appointed priests... (God) gave her no charge to minister baptism or bless disciples, nor did he bid her rule over the earth.[39]*

Christianity, as the orthodox understood it, was about the singular power of the Father, Son, and Holy Spirit, not about any feminine aspect of God.

Nevertheless, Marian worship persisted. When a council at Ephesus in 431 implied that Mary could be safely worshipped, crowds burst into delirious celebrations, accompanied by torchlight processions and shouts of "Praised be the Theotokos (Mother of God)!"[40] Older temples and sacred sites, once dedicated to pre-Christian goddesses, were rededicated or replaced with churches for Mary. In Rome on the Esquitine hill the Santa Maria Maggiore replaced Cybele's temple. Near the Pantheon a church dedicated to Mary adjoined Isis's sanctuary while another was built on a site which had been dedicated to Minerva. On the Capitoline in Aracoeli the Santa Maria supplanted a temple of the Phoenician goddess Tanit. In Cyprus, shrines that were Aphrodite's hallowed ground easily became those of Mary, who to this day is still called *Panaghia Aphroditessa*.[41] Geoffrey Ashe notes in *The Virgin*:

> *Like Cybele [Mary] guarded Rome. Like Athene she protected various other cities. Like Isis she watched over seafarers, becoming and remaining the 'Star of the Sea'. Like Juno she cared for pregnant women... She wore a crown recalling Cybele's. Enthroned with her child she resembled Isis with Horus. She even had touches of Neith about her.*[42]

The Church had not subdued veneration for feminine divinity; it had simply renamed it.

Interestingly, the Christian version of feminine divinity excluded any portrayal of one of the most powerful aspects of the Goddess, the face of the old, wise crone. Three faces of feminine divinity were common throughout pre-Christian traditions, that of the Virgin or Maiden, the Mother, and the Crone. Mary embodied the first two as both Virgin and Mother. The third face of the Crone, representing the culmination of feminine power and wisdom, was excluded from the Christian canon of saints. The Church's rejection of the Crone is significant in that it is precisely the Crone figure who later came to symbolize the ultimate enemy of the Church—the witch.

The Church reaped enormous gains by compromising its ideology and adapting to prevalent beliefs. In 319 Constantine passed a law excusing the clergy from paying taxes or serving in the army[43] and in 355 bishops were exempted from ever being tried in secular courts.[44] In 380 Emperor Theodosius passed a decree that read:

> *We shall believe in the single Deity of the Father, the Son, and the Holy Spirit, under the concept of equal majesty and of the Holy Trinity. 1. We command that those persons who follow*

this rule shall embrace the name of Catholic Christians. The rest, however, whom We adjudge demented and insane, shall sustain the infamy of heretical dogmas, their meeting places shall not receive the name of churches, and they shall be smitten first by divine vengeance and secondly by the retribution of Our own initiative, which We shall assume in accordance with the divine judgement.[45]

The Theodosian laws made it illegal to disagree with the Church. And a 388 prohibition forbade any public discussions of religious topics.

The ancient, multidimensional Pagan worship was prohibited in 392 and considered a criminal activity. In 410 the emperor Honorius decreed:

Let all who act contrary to the sacred laws know that their creeping in their heretical superstition to worship at the most remote oracle is punishable by exile and blood, should they again be tempted to assemble at such places for criminal activities...[46]

Pagan temples were pillaged and destroyed. A 386 written protest to the Roman government of Christian pillaging remains:

If they [the Christians] hear of a place with something worth raping away, they immediately claim that someone is making sacrifices there and committing abominations, and pay the place a visit—you can see them scurrying there, these guardians of good order (for that is what they call themselves), these brigands, if brigands is not too mild a word; for brigands at least try to conceal what they have done: if you call them brigands, they are outraged, but these people, on the contrary, show pride in their exploits... they believe they deserve rewards![47]

By 435 a law threatened any heretic in the Roman Empire with death. Judaism remained the only other legally recognized religion. Yet, Jews were isolated as much as possible, with intermarriage between Jew and Christian carrying the same penalty as adultery: the woman would be executed.[48] The Church had triumphed. The belief in but one face of God had led to the legal enforcement of but one religion.

Orthodox Christians acted on their belief about God. As they perceived God to control in an authoritarian manner, so they set about finding a way in which they, in God's name, could exercise similar authoritarian control. To that end, they built an organization that appealed to the government of the Roman Empire by promoting uniformity and obedience. In all likelihood, these Christians altered the story of Jesus's death in order to dissociate Christianity from rebellion against Roman authority. They established criteria that made it easy to recruit large numbers of people. The early Church compromised its ideology to accommodate contemporary beliefs. It was through political maneuvering that the Church won its standing as the official religion of the Roman Empire and the accompanying secular power and privilege.

ઢ ઢ ઢ

Chapter Three

Deciding upon Doctrine: Sex, Free Will, Reincarnation and the Use of Force

300 - 500 C.E.

The Church formulated its doctrine regarding sex, free will and reincarnation in response to early heretics. In each case, it chose ideological positions which best justified Church control over the individual and over society. The Church also developed a doctrine which justified its use of force in order to compel obedience. It was not long before the Church needed that doctrine to defend its violent suppression of heresy.

"Heresy" comes from the Greek *hairesis* meaning "choice."[1] In the early centuries there was much to choose from within Christianity—and consequently, many heresies. Gnostics were joined by Marcionites, Montanists, Arians, Sabellians, Nestorians, Monophysites, the Copts in Egypt, the Jacobites in Syria, and the Armenian Orthodox Church in disagreeing with the Catholic Church. The heresies surrounding Pelagius, Origen, and the Donatists led to particularly significant new doctrine. The Mannichaean heresy, while not leading to specific doctrine, set a precedent for the Church's denial of unpopular aspects of its own ideology.

The Pelagian controversy brought about Church doctrine regarding human free will and sexuality. Pelagius, an Irish monk who arrived in Rome at the beginning of the fifth century, believed that a person had freedom of will and responsibility for his or her actions. He believed that a person's own efforts play a part in determining whether or not he or she will be saved. In Pelagius's eyes, reliance upon redemption by Christ should be accompanied by individual responsibility and efforts to do good.[2] In granting humans responsibility for their acts, the Creator gave them freedom. As one historian writes:

Pelagius fought for the immeasurably precious good of man's freedom. That freedom cannot be surrendered without loss of human dignity... Unless man's freedom to make his own decisions is recognized, he is reduced to a mere marionette. According to Pelagius, the Creator conferred moral authority upon man, and to detract from that authority is to cast doubt upon man's likeness to God.[3]

Pelagius' most vehement opposition came from St. Augustine, the celebrated Doctor of the Church and Bishop of Hippo. Salvation, as Augustine saw it, is entirely in God's hands; there is nothing an individual can do. God has chosen but a few people to whom He will give bliss and salvation. It is for these few that Christ came into the world. All others are damned for all eternity. In Augustine's eyes, it is only God's grace and not any action or willingness on the part of the individual that leads to salvation.

Augustine believed that our freedom of will to choose good over evil was lost with the sin of Adam. Adam's sin, that, in Augustine's words, is in the "nature of the semen from which we were propagated," brought suffering and death into the world, took away our free will, and left us with an inherently evil nature.[4] To sin is now inevitable. Should we occasionally do good, it is only because of irresistible grace. "When, therefore, man lives according to man, not according to God, he is like the devil," Augustine wrote.[5] An individual, according to Augustine, has little power to influence his or her predetermined fate and is entirely dependent upon God for salvation.

Human sexuality, to Augustine, clearly demonstrates a human inability to choose good over evil. Augustine based this belief upon his own experience. Having himself led a promiscuous life in his youth during which he fathered and then abandoned an illegitimate child, he thought that sex was intrinsically evil. He complained of sexual desire:

> *Who can control this when its appetite is aroused? No one! In the very movement of this appetite, then, it has no 'mode' that responds to the decisions of the will... Yet what he wishes he cannot accomplish... In the very movement of the appetite, it has no mode corresponding to the decision of the will.[6]*

According to Augustine, human will is powerless either to indulge sexual desire or to suppress it:

> *But even those who delight in this pleasure are not moved to it at their own will, whether they confine themselves to lawful or transgress to unlawful pleasures; but sometimes this lust importunes them in spite of themselves, and sometimes fails them when they desire to feel it, so that though lust rages in the mind, it stirs not in the body. Thus, strangely enough, this emotion not only fails to obey the legitimate desire to beget offspring, but also refuses to serve lascivious lust; and though it often opposes its whole combined energy to the soul that resists it, sometimes also it is divided against itself, and while it moves the soul, leaves the body unmoved.[7]*

"This diabolical excitement of the genitals," as Augustine referred to sex, is evidence of Adam's original sin which is now transmitted "from the mother's womb," tainting all human beings with sin, and leaving them incapable of choosing good over evil or determining their own destiny.[8]

Augustine's views regarding sexuality differed sharply from pre-Christian views which often considered sex to be an integral part of the sacredness of life. His views did, however, represent those of many Christians. With the exception of minor heretical groups such as the Gnostic Carpocratians who exalted sex "as a bond between all created things,"[9] nearly all Christians thought that sex should be avoided except for purposes of procreation. St. Jerome warns, "Regard everything as poison which bears within it the seed of sensual pleasure."[10] In her book *Adam, Eve and the Serpent*, Elaine Pagels writes:

> *Clement (of Alexandria) excludes oral and anal intercourse, and intercourse with a menstruating, pregnant, barren, or menopausal wife and for that matter, with one's wife 'in the morning', 'in the daytime', or 'after dinner'. Clement warns, indeed, that 'not even at night, although in darkness, is it fitting to carry on immodestly or indecently, but with modesty, so that whatever happens, happens in the light of reason...' for even that union 'which is legitimate is still dangerous, except in so far as it is engaged in procreation of children.'[11]*

Sex as an act that empowers the individual threatens a religion intent upon controlling society. As Clement said, "lust is not easy to restrain, being devoid of fear..."[12]

Denying human free will and condemning sexual pleasure made it easier to control and contain people. Augustine wrote:

...man has been naturally so created that it is advantageous for him to be submissive, but disastrous for him to follow his own will, and not the will of his creator...[13]

He believed that Adam's "sin was a despising of the authority of God... it was just that condemnation followed..."[14] Augustine wrote to the bishop of Rome in 416, warning him that Pelagian ideas undermined the basis of episcopal authority and that appeasing the Pelagians would threaten the Catholic Church's new-found power.[15] Augustine's friend, the African bishop Alypius, brought 80 Numidian stallions to the imperial court as bribes to persuade the Church to side with Augustine against Pelagius. Augustine won. In April of 418 the pope excommunicated Pelagius. Ever since, the Catholic Church has officially embraced the doctrine of hereditary transmission of original sin.[16]

The Church formulated its position regarding reincarnation in response to the controversy surrounding Origen. Origen, a Christian scholar, thought that the human soul exists before it is incarnated into a physical body and then passes from one body to another until it is reunited with God, after which it no longer takes on a physical form. He believed that all souls eventually return to God. He thought that while Christ could greatly speed the reconciliation with God, such reconciliation would not take place without effort by the individual. Since humankind had fallen from God by its own free will, he argued, so humankind must also reunite with God through its own volition. The orthodox opposed Origen's theories, insisting that they depended too heavily upon individual self-determination.[17]

Orthodox Christians also thought the theory of reincarnation

3.1 St. Augustine, the much celebrated Father of the Church. His ideas and arguments gave the Church doctrines which denied human free will, condemned sex, and justified the use of force in order to compel obedience to the Church.

minimized the role of Jesus Christ, downplayed the necessity for salvation in this lifetime, and diminished the unique nature of Christ's resurrection. A person's salvation, in orthodox eyes, depends not upon self-determination and free will, as Origen's theories suggest, but only upon embracing Jesus Christ. Furthermore, if a person could choose to reunite with God in any one of many lifetimes, then there would be little fear of eternal damnation—and fear was deemed essential by the orthodox. Origen's idea that the soul is separable from the body also seemed to diminish the extraordinary nature of Christ's resurrection. The miracle of Christ's resurrection was understood to offer the possibility of overcoming *physical* death. If, however, each soul periodically overcomes death by separating from one body and entering into another, then Jesus's feat would not have been unique.

Origen's work also challenged the Church's control of intellectual and spiritual pursuit. Although he meticulously cited scripture to support his beliefs, Origen found that the scriptures provided limited direction in certain areas. Having received the education of a learned Greek, Origen continued to seek answers both in Platonic philosophy and in his own imagination when scripture was unavailing.[18] Augustine, too, had pondered questions to which scripture provided little guidance. Augustine asked, for example:

> ...and what before that life again, O God my
> joy, was I anywhere or in any body? For this I
> have none to tell me, neither father nor mother,
> nor experiences of others, nor mine own
> memory.[19]

Whereas Origen continued to contemplate and explore such questions, Augustine retreated from inquiry outside the scripture. He wrote:

> Either I would like to know those things of which
> I am ignorant as to the origin of the soul, or

else I should like to know if it is not for us to learn such things as long as we live here in this world. And yet, what if this is one of those things of which we are told: 'Seek not the things that are too high for thee, and search not into the things that are above thy ability: but the things that God hath commanded thee, think of them always and in many of his works be not curious.' (Ecclesiastes 3:22)[20]

Augustine went so far as to entertain the idea that before creating the world, God had busied Himself preparing a place of punishment for those with the audacity to question what had preceded creation.[21]

Although Origen died in 284, debate over his theories continued until 553 when he was officially anathematized, or cursed, by the Second Council of Constantinople. In condemning Origen, the Church indirectly dealt with the issue of reincarnation. Christians were not to believe in the pre-existence of souls, the existence of discarnate consciousness, or that a person has any more than this one lifetime to turn to the Christian God without being subject to eternal damnation. Furthermore, the anathemas against Origen served as another reminder that, regardless of the sincerity of one's faith, one should always remain within the ideological confines of scripture.

In dealing with the Donatist heresy, the Church set a precedent for using violence to suppress dissent. When the Donatists demanded higher standards of the clergy than the Catholic Church, their movement spread like wildfire, with Donatists outnumbering Catholics in Africa by the middle of the fourth century.[22] Having long maintained that no one should be forced to believe against his will, Augustine tried to bring the Donatists back into the Catholic fold through discussion. Yet, when the talks failed, he resorted to force, invoking the newly established Theodosian laws against heresy. The Church followed his advice and brutally crushed the Donatist movement.[23]

In opposing the Donatists, Augustine set forth the principle *Cognite intrare*, "Compel them to enter", that would be used throughout the middle ages to justify the Church's violent suppression of dissent and oppression of difference. Augustine contended:

> *The wounds of a friend are better than the kisses of an enemy. To love with sternness is better than to deceive with gentleness... In Luke 14:23 it is written: 'Compel people to come in!' By threats of the wrath of God, the Father draws souls to the Son.*[24]

Even at the beginning of the twentieth century Pope Leo XIII still argued that the ends justified the means:

> *The death sentence is a necessary and efficacious means for the Church to attain its end when rebels act against it and disturbers of the ecclesiastical unity, especially obstinate heretics and heresiarchs, cannot be restrained by any other penalty from continuing to derange the ecclesiastical order and impelling others to all sorts of crime... When the perversity of one or several is calculated to bring about the ruin of many of its children it is bound effectively to remove it, in such wise that if there be no other remedy for saving its people it can and must put these wicked men to death.*[25]

Another controversy, the Mannichaean heresy, demonstrated the Church's willingness to deny its own ideology when it was unpopular and unprofitable. Begun by the Persian Mani in the third century, Mannichaean theology is the logical consequence of the belief in singular supremacy. The belief in one all-powerful God often elicits the question of why there is pain and evil in the world. Why does an almighty God, who creates everything, create human suffering? The most common answer is that there must be a conflicting force, power, or god creating the evil; there must be a devil. A dualistic theology arises which understands life to be a struggle between God and satan, between good and evil, and between spirit and matter. The concept of a devil is exclusive to monotheism; evil is easier to understand and does not pose the need for a devil when there are many faces of God. In his book *Religion and the Decline of Magic*, Keith Thomas writes of early, pre-monotheistic Judaism:

> *The early Hebrews had no need to personify the principle of evil; they could attribute it to the influence of other rival deities. It was only the triumph of monotheism which made it necessary to explain why there should be evil in the world if God was good. The Devil thus helped to sustain the notion of an all-perfect divinity.*[26]

Mannichaeans embraced orthodox Christian ideology more completely than the early Catholic Church. They took the idea seriously that spirituality and godliness are detached from the physical world. The belief in a singular supremacy creates a hierarchy that separates its components, creating a division between heaven and earth, between spirit and matter. The components higher up on the hierarchy are considered good; the components lower down are considered evil. Accordingly, Mannichaeans advocated stringent asceticism and withdrawal from the world. Women, seen to tempt men with the earthly pleasures of sex and family, were considered to be part of satan's forces. To be closer to God, Mannichaeans believed that one must avoid anything that would bind one to earthly life.

Although the Church itself would adopt just such a Mannichaean theology centuries later during the Reformation, in the early years it could not politically afford to fully embrace such monotheism. The Church was struggling to incorporate vast numbers of people who still understood the world in a pagan, pantheistic and polytheistic context. Most people thought that everything within the physical world was imbued with a sense of the divine, that there was little separation between spirit and matter, and that divinity was personified in many different faces. To advocate a complete renunciation of the physical world as satan's realm and to abolish all but one divine persona would have led to certain failure in the Church's efforts to spread Christianity. So, although it still maintained the belief in a singular supremacy and in its implicit hierarchy, the Church also allowed worship of not only the Holy Virgin Mary, but also a multitude of angels and saints. Mannichaeanism may have been more consistent with orthodox ideology, but it was politically imprudent. Mannichaeans and all others who promoted similar ideas in the centuries that followed were labelled heretics.

The tenets formulated in response to early heretics lent doctrinal validation to the Church's control of the individual and society. By opposing Pelagius, the Church adopted Augustine's idea that people are inherently evil, incapable of choice, and thus in need of strong authority. Human sexuality is seen as evidence of their sinful nature. By castigating Origen's theories of reincarnation, the Church upheld its belief in the unique physical resurrection of Christ as well as the belief that a person has but one life in which to obey the Church or risk eternal damnation. With the Donatists, it established the precedent of using force to compel obedience. And with the Mannichaeans, the Church demonstrated its willingness to abandon its own beliefs for political expediency.

ಜಿ ಜಿ ಜಿ

Chapter Four

The Church Takes Over: The Dark Ages

500 - 1000 C.E.

The Church had devastating impact upon society. As the Church assumed leadership, activity in the fields of medicine, technology, science, education, history, art and commerce all but collapsed. Europe entered the Dark Ages. Although the Church amassed immense wealth during these centuries, most of what defines civilization disappeared.

The western Roman Empire fell during the fifth century under repeated attacks by the Germanic Goths and the Huns while the Roman province of Africa fell to the Vandals. Many blamed Christianity. In 410 when the Christian Visigoths sacked Rome, "the eternal city" which had held strong for 620 years, criticism of the new religion intensified. One of St. Augustine's most famous works, *The City of God*, was written as a defense of Christianity against such accusations.

However, the eastern Roman Empire, also called the Byzantine Empire, fared better. Especially under Emperor Justinian's rule (527-565), it recovered much of its power, regained control of Italy from the Ostrogoths and recovered Africa from the Vandals. Justinian and his wife, Theodora, were credited with the revival of literature, art, architecture, as well as the codification of Roman Law. But this flourishing Byzantine culture was cut short when the bubonic plague, beginning in 540, struck with a virulence unknown at any time in human history either before or since. In Byzantium alone, the plague was said to have claimed 10,000 people a day. The severity of this plague is difficult to fathom. The later Black Death of the 1300's, which some think killed one-third of Europe's population, claimed an estimated 27 million lives. In contrast, the sixth century plague is thought to have taken 100 million lives.[1] The Roman Empire never recovered.

The plague had quite different impact upon Christianity. People flocked to the Church in terror.[2] The Church explained that the plague was an act of God, and disease a punishment for the sin of not obeying Church authority. The Church branded Justinian a heretic. It declared the field of Greek and Roman medicine, useless in fighting the plague, to be heresy.[3] While the plague assured the downfall of the Roman Empire, it strengthened the Christian church.

After the plague, the Church dominated the formal discipline of medicine. The most common medical practice between the sixth and sixteenth centuries used for every malady became "bleeding." Christian monks taught that bleeding a person would prevent toxic imbalances, prevent sexual desire, and restore the humors. By the sixteenth century this practice would kill tens of thousands each year. Yet, when a person died during blood-letting, it was only lamented that treatment had not been started sooner and performed more aggressively.[4]

Technology disappeared as the Church became the most cohesive power in Western society. The extensive aqueduct and plumbing systems vanished. Orthodox Christians taught that all aspects of the flesh should be reviled and therefore discouraged washing as much as possible. Toilets and indoor plumbing disappeared. Disease became commonplace as sanitation and

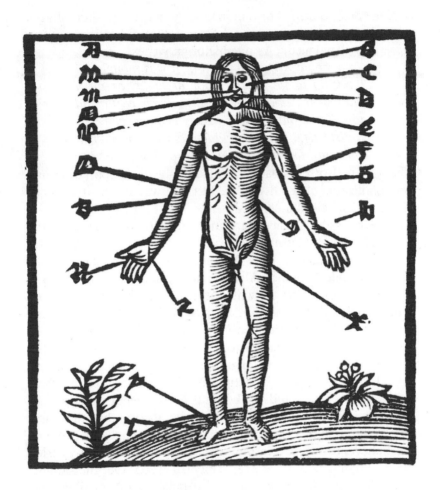

4.1   Once the fields of Greek and Roman medicine were declared
heretical, the dangerous medical practice of bleeding became common.
This engraving published in 1516 illustrates the points from which blood
was to be let.

hygiene deteriorated. For hundreds of years, towns and villages were decimated by epidemics.[5] Roman central heating systems were also abandoned.[6] As one historian writes:

> From about A.D. 500 onward, it was thought no hardship to lie on the floor at night, or on a hard bench above low drafts, damp earth and rats. To be indoors was luxury enough. Nor was it distasteful to sleep huddled closely together in company, for warmth was valued above privacy.[7]

The vast network of roads that had enabled transportation and communication also fell into neglect and would remain so until almost the nineteenth century.[8]

The losses in science were monumental. In some cases the Christian church's burning of books and repression of intellectual pursuit set humanity back as much as two millennia in its scientific understanding. Already in the sixth century B.C.E., Pythagoras had come up with the idea that the earth revolved around the sun. By the third century B.C.E., Aristarchus had outlined the heliocentric theory and Eratosthenes had measured the circumference of the Earth. By the second century B.C.E., Hipparchus had invented longitude and latitude and had determined the obliquity of the ecliptic.[9] After the onset of the Dark Ages, however, it would not be until the sixteenth century C.E. that Copernicus would reintroduce the theory that the earth revolves around the sun. And when Galileo attempted to promote the heliocentric theory in the seventeenth century, he was tried by the Inquisition in Rome. Only in 1965 did the Roman Catholic Church revoke its condemnation of Galileo. St. Augustine echoed the Church's scientific understanding of the world:

> It is impossible there should be inhabitants on the opposite side of the earth, since no such race is recorded by Scripture among the descendants of Adam.[10]

History was rewritten to become a verification of Christian beliefs. Orthodox Christians thought history necessary only in order to place the events of the past into Biblical context. In Daniel Boorstin's words, "History became a footnote to ortho-doxy."[11] He writes in his book *The Discoverers*:

The Christian test was a willingness to believe in the one Jesus Christ and His Message of salva-tion. What was demanded was not criticism but credulity. The Church Fathers observed that in the realm of thought only heresy had a history.[12]

Eusebius of Caesarea set about during the time of Constantine to rewrite the history of the world into a history of Christianity:

'Other writers of history,' Eusebius wrote, recorded the fighting of wars waged 'for the sake of children and country and other posses-sions. But our narrative of the government of God will record in ineffaceable letters the most peaceful wars waged in behalf of the peace of the soul...'[13]

Blind faith replaced the spirit of historical investigation. One should trust, as Eusebius said, "the incontrovertible words of the Master to his disciples: 'It is not for you to know the times or the seasons, which the Father hath put in his own power.'"[14]

Although the Church restricted historical inquiry more severely, it carried on a process of rewriting history that had started much earlier. Twentieth century archeology is beginning to reveal a very different picture of human history than may have been told even in pre-Christian Rome. The idea that history began only 5,000 years ago is terribly inaccurate. During the neolithic age after people had turned from hunting and gathering to agriculture, particularly between 7000 B.C.E. and 4000 B.C.E., cultures of startling sophistication flourished. Art, architecture, city-planning, dance, ritual drama, trade both by land and sea, writing, law and government were well-known to these peoples. The first ideas of democracy originally date back not to the Greeks but far earlier to this neolithic age. Perhaps most remarkable is that these cultures show no evidence of hierarchy as we know it; they knew no war, organized oppression or slavery.[15]

Rewriting history to erase awareness of such a past helped those in power deflect criticism for the current state of affairs. Portraying human society as having steadily evolved rather than having experienced major setbacks gives the impression that, however ugly and violent society may be now, it was even more savage in the past. Augustine's disciple, Orosius, for instance, in his *Seven Books of Histories against the Pagans*, demonstrated that the evils of the time could not be blamed on Christianity because earlier times had experienced even worse calamities.[16] Distorting and rewriting history gave the impression that Christianity had not only lifted society from harsher, more barbaric times, but that a social structure of hierarchy and domination had always existed and was therefore inevitable.

The Christian church had similar impact upon education and learning. The Church burned enormous amounts of literature. In 391 Christians burned down one of the world's greatest libraries in Alexandria, said to have housed 700,000 rolls.[17] All the books of the Gnostic Basilides, Porphyry's 36 volumes, papyrus rolls of 27 schools of the Mysteries, and 270,000 ancient documents gathered by Ptolemy Philadelphus were burned.[18] Ancient academies of learning were closed. Education for anyone outside of the Church came to an end. And what little education there was during the Dark Ages, while still limited to the clergy, was advocated by powerful kings as a means of providing themselves with capable administrators.[19]

4.2 As the Church grew more powerful, Christians closed academies and burned books as well as whole libraries. This engraving depicts converts to St. Paul burning books.

The Church opposed the study of grammar and Latin. Pope Gregory I, or Gregory the Great, a man thought to have been one of the greatest architects of the medieval order,[20] objected to grammatical study. He wrote:

> *I despise the proper constructions and cases, because I think it very unfitting that the words of the celestial oracle should be restricted by the rules of Donatus [a well-known grammarian].*[21]

Gregory the Great also condemned education for all but the clergy as folly and wickedness. He forbade laymen to read even the Bible. He had the library of the Palatine Apollo burned "lest its secular literature distract the faithful from the contemplation of heaven."[22]

The Fourth Council of Carthage in 398 forbade bishops to even read the books of gentiles.[23] Jerome, a Church Father and early monastic in the fourth century, rejoiced that the classical authors were being forgotten. And his younger monastic contemporaries were known to boast of their ignorance of everything except Christian literature.[24] After Christians had spent years destroying books and libraries, St. John Chrysostom, the preeminent Greek Father of the Church, proudly declared, "Every trace of the old philosophy and literature of the ancient world has vanished from the face of the earth."[25]

Monastic libraries, the only libraries left, were composed of books of devotion. Even the most significant monastic libraries carried little aside from books about Christian theology.[26] While monks did copy manuscripts, such work was not esteemed for its intrinsic value but rather considered part of the prescribed manual labor, necessary in the effort of "fighting the Devil by pen and ink," in the words of the Christian Cassiodorus.[27]

4.3   St. Gregory the Great, Pope from 590-604. While best known for strengthening the Pope's independence from the Byzantine Emperor, he also burned books and restricted reading and education to the clergy.

Copying manuscripts, even if those manuscripts were classical, did not necessarily indicate an appreciation for classical learning. An historian notes that the order of Cluni followed customs that implied a lack of respect for classical works. "If a monk wanted a book during the hours of silence, he made a sign of turning the leaves; if he wanted a classical book, he scratched his ear like a dog."[28]

The Church had devastating impact upon artistic expression. According to orthodox Christianity, art should enhance and promote Christian values; it should not serve simply as an individual's creative exploration and expression. New works of art which did not concur with the Church's ideology would not be created again until the Renaissance. Marble statues of ancient Rome were torn down, most notably by Gregory the Great, and made into lime. Architectural marbles and mosaics were either made into lime or went to adorn cathedrals all over Europe and as far away as Westminster Abbey in London. The ravaging of marble works accounts for the thin ornate slabs with ancient inscriptions still found in many churches today.[29]

The rise of the Christian church coincided with a severe economic collapse throughout the western world. The Church did little to encourage trade. The canons of Gratian include a sixth century document which states, "Whoever buys a thing in order to re-sell it intact, no matter what it is, is like the merchant driven from the Temple."[30] The Church stigmatized lending money at interest, which made funding economic ventures extremely difficult. Commercial contracts of the time indicate that the Church would sometimes intervene and free a debtor from liabilities, undermining even further the likelihood of anyone wanting to lend money.[31]

The Church itself, however, was one of the few profitable organizations of the time. As such, it provided a potentially lucrative occupation for many men. Money and power played a critical role in a man's ascent through the Church hierarchy and contributed to the disreputable nature of the medieval Church. At least forty different Popes are known to have bought their way into the papacy.[32] Allegations of murder and crime within the Church abounded as the papacy so frequently changed hands. In a particular one hundred year period, more than forty Popes came to office. In the twelve year period from 891 to 903 alone, no less than ten different Popes held power.[33]

The Church amassed inordinate wealth during the Dark Ages. Patrimonial properties, the Church-held lands that were free and clear of taxes or military obligation to the king, made up between one-quarter and one-third of western Europe.[34] In addition to patrimony, bishops often held territories in feudal tenure, obliging them like any count or baron to provide the king with soldiers when called. The Church made money by collecting revenues from imperial rulers, by confiscating property as the result of court judgments, by selling the remission of sins (called "indulgences"), by selling ecclesiastical offices (called "simony"), and sometimes by simply taking land by force.[35]

Alliances with the state were essential to the Church's secular influence and wealth. However, unlike during the Roman Empire, several imperial forces now held power. By the year 700, for example, the West was divided into four political realms. Spain was ruled by the Christian Visigoths and would fall in 711-713 to the Islamic Moors. Anglo-Saxons ruled England. The Franks ruled Gaul. Italy was held primarily by the Lombards with a few regions still in the hands of the Byzantine Empire.[36] The new, more complicated alliance between the Church and various imperial rulers came to be known as the Holy Roman Empire and was best symbolized by the Pope's crowning of Charlemagne in 800 and the German king, Otto I, in 952.

Both Church and state profited from their alliance. Imperial rulers provided not only military resources but also lucrative positions for the clergy. By overseeing the administrative matters of rulers, bishops became vested with both military and civil authority. They came to be as powerful and as influential as the greatest of feudal lords. The historian Jeffrey Burton Russell writes:

> *The system was self-perpetuating: the more power and wealth the bishops had, the more the kings needed to appoint loyal men; but to secure and preserve the loyalty of such men, the kings had to bestow upon them further power and wealth. It is no wonder that the bishops kept their eyes more attentively upon the throne than upon the cross.*[37]

In an age when the belief in the divine right of kings prevailed, the Pope's support of a king was thought to be essential. The Church also brought a semblance of unity to an imperial realm by converting its people to Christianity.

These widespread conversions, however, were usually little more than a facade. Pope Gregory I in a letter to his emissary to Britain, St. Augustine of Canterbury, illustrates his concern with the appearance that people had converted to Christianity:

> *...the people will have no need to change their place of concourse; where of old they were wont to sacrifice cattle to demons, thither let them continue to resort on the day of the Saint to whom the Church is dedicated, and slay their beasts, no longer as a sacrifice to demons, but for a social meal in honour of Him whom they now worship.*[38]

Although the medieval Church wrought havoc in most arenas of life, it did not effect real change in the way common people perceived God. The Church's continual admonishments against pagan practices indicate how insubstantial most conversions to Christianity were. It constantly warned against customs relating to trees, nature and the belief in magic, occasionally going so far as to raze a church after discovering that people were actually worshipping older gods or goddesses there.[39] A 742 Church decree read:

> ...every pagan defilement should be rejected and spurned, whether it be sacrifices of the dead, or soothsaying and divining, or amulets and omens, or incantations, or the offering of sacrifices—by (all of) which ignorant people perform pagan rites alongside those of the church, under cover of the names of the sacred martyrs and confessors.[40]

Sacred springs were renamed in honor of saints and churches built over the sites of pagan temples, yet the nature of reverence and worship remained unchanged.

The Church played a critical role in taking Europe into the Dark Ages. Its devastating impact was felt in nearly every sphere of human endeavor. Ironically, the one area where the medieval Church had little profound impact was in changing the spirituality of common people. While most people adopted a Christian veneer, they did not significantly change their understanding or perception of God.

ða. ða. ða.

Chapter Five

The Church Fights Change: The Middle Ages

1000 - 1500 C.E.

The spirit of the Middle Ages challenged the Church's now-established authority. The Church responded by bolstering its authoritarian structure, asserting the Pope's supremacy over all imperial powers, and rallying Europe against Muslims, Jews and Eastern Orthodox Christians. When the crusades failed to unify Europe under its control, the Church attacked whomever it perceived as an enemy: money-lenders, supporters of nation-states, and the Cathars.

Dramatic changes after the turn of the millennium ushered in the high Middle Ages. An agricultural society began to give way to rapidly growing towns as the population exploded in a surge unparalleled in the Western world until the 19th and 20th centuries.[1] Many more people began making their livelihoods in commerce and industry, giving rise to a new social class of traders and manufacturers.[2] These merchants often served as examples that through wit, activity and industry one could change one's lot in life. Merchants also disseminated new information and ideas from the Arab and Greek worlds as they traveled along trade routes from northern Spain and southern

Italy.

Latin classics, largely lost under Christian rule, were translated from Arabic back into Latin. When Aristotle's work was reintroduced to the West, its example of systematic thought spawned scholasticism, a discipline that challenged the Church's demand that one accept its assertions on blind faith. The twelfth century Peter Abelard, for example, used the scholastic method to encourage individual decision-making, to question authoritarian assertions, and to point out contradictions in Church doctrine and scripture.

The Church's confinement of all education and creativity to monasteries began to break down. Not only were lay schools created to provide elementary education to merchant and artisan classes, but universities were formed in urban areas such as Paris, Oxford, Toulouse, Montpellier, Cambridge, Salerno, Bologna and Salamanca.[3] The age saw literary epics and romances such as *The Romance of the Rose*, *The Song of the Cid*, *Arthur's Knights of the Round Table*, the *Nibelungenlied*, and Dante's *Divine Comedy*.[4] Court jesters or fools provided contemporary sources of vernacular poetry and literature. Renewed interest in architecture produced the culmination of the Romanesque style and the beginning of Gothic artistic and engineering feats. Even within twelfth century monasteries, the art of illumination and ornamentation of manuscripts came alive.[5] Art, literature, philosophy and architecture all began to flourish again during the high Middle Ages.

Having prospered and thrived while society remained subdued and quiescent, the Church now resisted the many changes taking place. Papal prohibitions in 1210 and 1215 restricted the teaching of Aristotle's works in Paris. By 1272 discussion of any purely theological matter was forbidden.[6] St. Bernard of Clairvaux gave voice to Church sentiment when he said of Abelard's scholasticism, "everything (is) treated contrary to custom and tradition." Bernard wrote:

*The faith of simplicity is mocked, the secrets of
Christ profaned; questions on the highest things
are impertinently asked, the Fathers scorned
because they were disposed to conciliate rather
than solve such problems. Human reason is
snatching everything to itself, leaving nothing for
faith.*[7]

The Church demonstrated a similar disdain for the revival of
classical literature. As the twelfth century Christian Honorius of
Autun asked:

*How is the soul profited by the strife of Hector,
the arguments of Plato, the poems of Virgil, or
the elegies of Ovid, who, with others like them,
are now gnashing their teeth in the prison of the
infernal Babylon, under the cruel tyranny of
Pluto?*[8]

The Church regarded poetry with particular disfavor, sometimes
classifying poets with magicians whom the Church despised. The
illustrations in the twelfth century *Hortus deliciarum* of Herrad
of Landsberg, for example, depict four "poets or magicians,"
each with an evil spirit prompting him.[9] Clerics insisted that
court jesters also "have no use or virtue" and are "beyond hope
of salvation."[10]

Orthodox Christians expressed disdain for the flourishing
creativity and declared supporters of the arts to be heathens and
pagans. The outspoken fifteenth century Dominican prophet
Girolamo Savonarola believed that classical poets should be
banished and that science, culture and education should return
entirely to the hands of monks. He wrote:

*The only good thing that we owe to Plato and
Aristotle is that they brought forward many
arguments which we can use against the heretics. Yet they and other philosophers are now in
hell... It would be good for religion if many*

books that seem useful were destroyed. When there were not so many books and not so many arguments and disputes, religion grew more quickly than it has since.[11]
Savonarola carried out his moral reforms in Florence using techniques characteristic of a police state: controlling personal morality through the espionage of servants and organizing bands of young men to raid homes of items that were inconsistent with orthodox Christian ideals. Books, particularly those of Latin and Italian poets, illuminated manuscripts, women's ornaments, musical instruments, and paintings were burned in a huge bonfire in 1497, destroying much of the work of Renaissance Florence.

Yet medieval society abounded with dissent. Many began to seek a relationship with God outside of the Church. Common people in the Middle Ages found little in the Church to which they could relate. Churches had become grander and more formal, sharply emphasizing the difference between the clergy and laity. In some churches, a choir screen would even segregate the congregation from the altar. The language of the Mass, which in the fourth century had been changed from Greek to Latin so as to be more easily understood, was by the end of the seventh century totally incomprehensible to most people, including many priests. As a result, services were often an unintelligible mumbling which was absolutely meaningless to the congregation.[12]

The Church, now enormously wealthy, interested itself more in collecting money than in relating to its members. The medieval Church's preoccupation with riches was such that its ten commandments were said to have been reduced to one: "Bring hither the money."[13] Priests were selected more on the basis of their money than upon any other virtue. A huge disparity developed not only between the clergy and the laity but also between ranks of the clergy. The income of a wealthy bishop, for example, could range from 300 times to as much as

1000 times that of a vicar.[14] In the twelfth century the Church forbade clergy to marry in order to prevent property from passing out of the Church to the families of clergy.[15] The incongruity of an extravagantly wealthy organization representing the ideals of Jesus Christ prompted the papal bull or edict *Cum inter nonnullos* in 1326 which proclaimed it heresy to say that Jesus and his Apostles owned no property.[16]

Those seeking a more meaningful connection with God increasingly turned to movements outside the Catholic Church. These medieval heresies exhibited great diversity of thought. There were apocalyptic sects that were convinced that the world was coming to an end, such as those led by Tanchelin, Peter de Bruys, Henry of Lausanne, and Arnold of Brescia. Other groups such as the Waldensians and Lollards foreshadowed the Protestants in their desire for a stricter adherence to Christian scripture. And yet other groups like the Brethren of the Free Spirit, the Tulupins, and the Adamites embraced pantheistic and animistic beliefs that perceived the physical world to be wholly imbued with God's presence.[17] At the turn of the fourteenth century, Meister Eckhart challenged the very need for a Church. He wrote, "When the Kingdom appears to the soul and it is recognized, there is no further need for preaching or instruction."[18]

Many heretics insisted upon a direct relationship with God. Despite the danger, they translated the Bible into common or vernacular languages which lay people could understand. Simple possession of such a Bible was punishable by death.[19] In the spirit of providing images to which people could relate, the portrayal of Christ also became more human and accessible. From Romanesque depictions of Jesus as the stiff, hieratic, and unapproachable judge of the universe, Gothic art now portrayed him as more of a suffering, compassionate human being.[20]

The cult of the Virgin blossomed in the Middle Ages. The Virgin Mary became a figure to whom one could turn for forgiveness and who could protest God's judgment and unrelenting law. In his book *The Virgin*, Geoffrey Ashe tells of the stories which illustrate her kindness and compassion:

> *A thief prays to her before going out to rob, and when he is hanged, she sustains him in the air till the hangman acknowledges the miracle and lets him live.*
>
> *A nun who leaves her convent to plunge into vice, but keeps praying to Mary, returns at last to find that Mary has taken her place and no one has missed her.*[21]

Complete litanies were devoted to the Virgin Mary. The grandest of medieval cathedrals were dedicated to her: at Paris, Chartres, Reims, Amiens, Rouen, Bayeux, Coutances, Noyon, and Laon.[22] She developed names like "spiritual vessel," "cause of our joy," "Ark of the Covenant" and "Seat of Wisdom." Chaucer refers to her as the "almighty and all merciful Queen."[23] A painted wooden figure of the Madonna and child by a fourteenth century German artist gives an indication of medieval veneration for this female image of divinity. When her figure is opened, the Madonna is shown to contain the whole Trinity.[24]

The Church responded, not by trying to meet people's needs, but by strengthening its own authoritarian structure, developing its own judicial system, and more forcefully asserting its supremacy over all. The papacy expanded its administrative and advisory council called the curia, increased its regulation of bishops, began again to summon councils, and, most significantly, used papal legates. Papal legates were officers who could override the authority of bishops and archbishops, effectively eroding the local authority of bishops and bringing the monasteries more directly under papal control.[25]

The Church developed its own system of law to claim authority in secular matters. The revival of civil law, derived from Roman and Germanic law, had been replacing many feudal

OPPOSITE: Figure 5.1 This fifteenth century woodcut illustrates the nurturing and protective nature attributed to the Virgin Mary.

ABOVE: Figure 5.2 This woodcut, also from the fifteenth century, similarly depicts the Madonna as a protectress. With the help of angels, she shelters people from God's arrows.

customs and facilitating trade by implementing principles with wider application than rural customs which could differ with each locale.[26] Roman law, however, did not recognize the Pope. By 1149 St. Bernard had realized the implicit threat of civil law to the Church and complained that the courts rang with Justinian's laws rather than those of God.[27] By 1219 the Pope had forbidden priests to study Roman law and had altogether prohibited its teaching at the University of Paris.[28]

Instead, the Church drew up its own system called canon law. The eleventh century Ivo of Chartres and the twelfth century Gratian reworked the bulk of uncoordinated and often conflicting decrees and letters into comprehensive codes that asserted the Pope's supremacy. Should the Pope himself find these laws inconvenient, however, he was allowed under these same canon laws to dispense with them at any time. Ecclesiastical tribunals claimed jurisdiction over all cases in which Church interests were at stake such as those concerning tithes, benefices, donations and wills. To protect its own, the Church claimed the right to try all members of the clergy.[29] The Church also claimed jurisdiction over any matter pertaining to a sacrament or an oath. As one historian points out, "there was scarcely a limit to [the Church's] intervention; for in medieval society wellnigh everything was connected with a sacrament or depended upon an oath."[30]

Many of the Church's efforts at systematizing and adding credence to canon law focused upon establishing the Pope's supremacy over imperial powers. The theory of the "plentitude of power" gave the Pope as the vicar of Christ full authority over both secular and spiritual affairs. It allowed him to prohibit the distribution of sacraments within an imperial realm and to both excommunicate and depose a king.[31] Dictates of canon law invalidated the ordination of imperially appointed Popes, called anti-popes, and any members of the clergy ordained as a result of such imperially appointed Popes.

Ancient letters were "discovered" and incorporated into canon law as evidence of the Pope's supremacy over imperial powers. One such letter, the "Donation of Constantine," purported to be a letter from Emperor Constantine to Pope Sylvester in which Constantine attributes his power to the Pope. It reads, "We give to... Sylvester, the Universal Pope... the city of Rome and all the provinces, districts, and cities of Italy and the Western regions..."[32] By the sixteenth century these letters were exposed as total forgeries.

The Pope became increasingly involved in directing political conflicts and the conquering of lands. Pope Boniface VIII wrote to the Hapsburg Albert of Austria, "We donate to you, in the plentitude of our power, the kingdom of France, which belongs of right to the Emperors of the West."[33] In his letter to King Henry II of England, the twelfth century Pope Adrian IV sanctioned the English invasion of Ireland. He wrote:

> It is not doubted, and you know it, that Ireland and all those islands which have received the faith, belong to the Church of Rome; if you wish to enter that Island, to drive vice out of it, to cause law to be obeyed and St. Peter's Pence to be paid by every house, it will please us to assign it to you.[34]

Historian Phillip Schaff describes the actions of the medieval papacy:

> To depose princes, to absolve subjects from allegiance, to actively foment rebellion as against Frederick II, to divert lands as in Southern France, to give away crowns, to extort by threat of the severest ecclesiastical penalties the payment of tribute, to punish religious dissenters with perpetual imprisonment or turn them over to the secular authorities, knowing death would be the punishment, to send and consecrate

crusading armies, and to invade the realm of the
civil court, usurp its authority, and annul a
nation's code, as in the case of Magna Charta,
—these were the high prerogatives actually
exercised by the papacy.[35]

Papal desire for power grew insatiable. Seeing themselves as superior to all other mortals, Popes claimed not only that every person was subject to papal authority, but that the Pope himself was accountable to no one but God. In 1302 Pope Boniface issued the bull *Unam Sanctam*:

Therefore, if the earthly power errs, it shall be
judged by the spiritual power... but if the su-
preme spiritual power errs it can be judged only
by God, and not by man... Therefore we de-
clare, state, define and pronounce that it is
altogether necessary to salvation for every
human creature to be subject to the Roman
pontiff.[36]

Understandably, arguments erupted over who would be Pope and hold such power. In what was called the Great Schism, two separate lines of Popes, one living in Rome and one in Avignon, reigned from 1378 to 1417. They disagreed, not over matters concerning Christian ideology or religious practices, but over politics and who should reign.

Another means with which the Church responded to the time was an attempt to focus attention away from the tumultuous social changes and towards an outside enemy. In 1095 Pope Urban II called for the knights of Europe to unite and march to Jerusalem to save the holy land from the Islamic infidel. The crusades provided an opportunity to vastly increase the influence of the Catholic Church. They also served a political purpose much closer to home. When the Pope initiated the first crusade in 1095, many of the imperial powers were outside the Church: the King of France, the King of England, and the German

Emperor.[37] The crusades were a means of uniting much of Europe in the name of Christianity.

Crusaders, caught up in their sense of righteousness, brutally attacked the Church's enemies. Pope Gregory VII had declared, "Cursed be the man who holds back his sword from shedding blood."[38] The chronicler, Raymond of Aguilers, described the scene when a band of crusaders massacred both Muslims and Jews in Jerusalem in 1099:

> *Wonderful things were to be seen. Numbers of the Saracens were beheaded... Others were shot with arrows, or forced to jump from the towers; others were tortured for several days, then burned with flames. In the streets were seen piles of heads and hands and feet. One rode about everywhere amid the corpses of men and horses. In the temple of Solomon, the horses waded in the blood up to their knees, nay, up to the bridle. It was a just and marvelous judgement of God, that this place should be filled with the blood of unbelievers.[39]*

Nicetas Choniates, a Byzantine chronicler, wrote, "Even the Saracens (the Muslims) are merciful and kind compared to these men who bear the cross of Christ on their shoulders."[40]

Another enemy targeted by the crusades was the Eastern Church based in Constantinople. The cultures of the East and West had been growing apart for centuries. Having upheld more respect for the arts, literature and education, Eastern culture seemed more sophisticated than the West. The East had reverently preserved the writings of the ancient Greeks. Greek remained the official language of law, government, the Eastern church, and Eastern literature. In the West, however, even the Greek alphabet was lost. As the historian Charles H. Haskins writes, "at the hands of the medieval scribe a Greek word becomes gibberish or is omitted with *grecum* inserted in its

POPE URBAN PREACHING THE CRUSADES.

place—it was "all Greek" to him."[41] Starting in the late 700's the two cultures began to use different coinage.[42] Disparity between the two cultures grew as the churches each developed their own forms of Christian rites. They celebrated Easter on different days. They differed in their views regarding the use of icons, and in the ordering of the Holy Trinity in the Nicene Creed.[43] There was little that the East and West now shared in common other than that they both considered themselves Christian.

In 1054, after attempts at reconciling the differences between Rome and Constantinople failed, the two branches of Christianity formalized their separation. To a Roman Church that vigorously asserted its supremacy over all, however, such a separation was seen as an affront to and a rejection of the Pope's authority. With the help of priests who encouraged the idea that the schismatic Greeks were satan's henchmen and were to blame for every misfortune, the People's Crusade of 1096 sacked Belgrade, the chief imperial city after Constantinople.[44] A Greek chronicler wrote of the Pope:

> ...he wished to compel us to recognize the
> Pope's primacy among all prelates and to com-
> memorate his name in public prayers, under
> pain of death against those who refuse.[45]

Later in 1204 Pope Innocent III sent a group of crusaders to Constantinople. The soldiers of Christ fell upon Constantinople with a vengeance, raping, pillaging and burning the city.[46] According to the chronicler Geoffrey Villehardouin, never since the creation of the world had so much booty been taken from a city.[47] The Pope's response to the Greek Emperor:

> ...we believe that the Greeks have been punished
> through (the Crusades) by the just judgement of

5.3 Pope Urban preaching the crusades. While the ostensible purpose of the crusades was to rescue the holy land from the infidel, the crusades also helped unify Europeans under the banner of Christianity and avert criticism from the papacy.

God: these Greeks who have striven to rend the
Seamless Robe of Jesus Christ... Those who
would not join Noah in his ark perished justly in
the deluge; and these have justly suffered famine
and hunger who would not receive as their
shepherd the blessed Peter, Prince of the
Apostles...[48]

To the Pope, the rape of Constantinople was just punishment for not submitting to the Roman Catholic Church. Biblical passages supported his stance: "But those mine enemies, which would not that I should reign over them, bring hither, and slay them before me."[49]   Following the attack, a Latin patriarch subject to the Pope ruled the domain until 1261.[50] Constantinople, however, was left severely weakened and in 1453 fell to Turkish conquest.

In the roughly 200 years of crusades, thousands, if not millions, were killed. Invading crusaders destroyed in much the same way as the Church had at the onset of the Dark Ages. They burned any books they found.[51] Hebrew scrolls such as 12,000 volumes of the Talmud and the works of Maimonides were burned.[52] While they pillaged and looted with a vengeance, crusaders were often unable to transport anything upon the difficult journey home. Although the crusades did bring about moments of solidarity as Europeans rallied together in the name of Christianity, they fell far short of all their other intentions. The crusades failed to gain more than fleeting control of Jerusalem, and failed to enrich their crusaders. Far from gaining converts to the Roman Catholic Church, the crusades spread a bitter animosity that still lingers today.[53]

European Jews were often the first victims of a crusade. But Christian persecution of Jews continued long after the crusades ended. Jews became the scapegoats for many problems that the Church could not fix. When, for example, the black death, the

---

5.4 A depiction of Crusaders entering Constantinople.

bubonic plague, struck in the fourteenth century, the Church explained that Jews were to blame and prompted attacks upon them.[54] A whole folklore developed claiming that Jews kidnapped and ate Christian children in Jewish rituals of cannibalism, and that Jews stole and profaned the blessed Christian sacraments. These were the same tales that Romans once told of the hated Christians, the same tales that Christians would tell of witches, and the same tales Protestants would tell of Catholics.[55] Pogroms, the raiding and destroying of Jewish synagogues and ghettos, became a common demonstration of Christian righteousness.

Jews were easy targets for they had never been embraced by Christian society. Under the feudal system, a ceremony of investiture involving a Christian oath excluded Jews from working the land and sent them into commerce and crafts in the towns. However, with the rapid population expansion of the eleventh and twelfth centuries and the consequent influx of people to the cities, artisan guilds were established, each with its own patron saint. Jews were again driven from the crafts into what fields remained: banking, money-changing and money-lending.[56] Persecuting Jews, therefore, also became a convenient means of getting rid of one's creditors. Religious arguments were taken up by indebted kings to justify their confiscation of Jewish property and their expulsion of Jews from their domains.[57]

Anyone who held power became a likely target for the Church. The Knights Templar, a group originally formed to protect crusaders, gained political influence and became known as trustworthy moneylenders.[58] They were also thought to have brought back with them Gnostic, Kabalistic, and Islamic mysteries. Threatened by the Templars' growing political power, suspicious of their seemingly independent religious beliefs, and jealous of their wealth, both Church and kings had reason to persecute them. As with the Jews, incredible stories began to circulate about the Templars, including accounts of an initiation ritual which involved denying Christ, God, and the Virgin, and spitting, trampling and urinating upon the cross. Accused of homosexuality, of killing illegitimate children, and of witchcraft, the Templars were murdered and their property confiscated.[59]

The Church found itself at odds with a seemingly endless array of people in the Middle Ages. It reacted swiftly and forcefully to suppress the first seeds of nationalism and desire for independence from Rome. When disputes over tribute payments arose in 1275, the Pope excommunicated the whole town of Florence.[60] And, when a group of smaller Italian city-states organized a revolt against papal control in 1375, the Pope's legate in Italy, Robert of Geneva, hired a mercenary band to reconquer the area. After failing to take the city of Bologna, this band set upon the smaller town of Cessna.[61]

> *Swearing clemency by a solemn oath on his cardinal's hat, Cardinal Robert persuaded the men of Cessna to lay down their arms, and won their confidence by asking for 50 hostages and immediately releasing them as evidence of good will. Then summoning his mercenaries... he ordered a general massacre 'to exercise justice.'*
> *... For three days and nights beginning February 3, 1377, while the city gates were closed, the soldiers slaughtered. 'All the squares were full of dead.' Trying to escape, hundreds drowned in the moats, thrust back by relentless swords. Women were seized for rape, ransom was placed on children, plunder succeeded the killing, works of art were ruined, handicrafts laid waste, 'and what could not be carried away, they burned, made unfit for use or spilled upon the ground.'*
> *The toll of the dead was between 2,500-5000.*[62]

Robert of Geneva was appointed Pope three years later in 1378 and became Clement VII.[63]

Judging by the ferocity of its attack upon a group called the Cathars, the Church was more grandly threatened by this heresy than by any other in history. Catharism thrived in southern France, an area then known as Langedoc. Politically and culturally distinct from the north, Langedoc was tolerant of difference. Many races lived together harmoniously—Greeks, Phoenicians, Jews and Muslims. Jews were not only free from persecution, but held management and advisory positions with lords and even prelates. There was less class distinction, a milder form of serfdom, freer towns, and a judicial system based upon Roman law.[64] Nowhere were citizens as educated.[65] Culture and commerce flourished, making it one of the most prosperous regions in Europe.

Catharism incorporated diverse religious elements. There is evidence of a strong connection between Catharism, Moslem Sufi communities and the Jewish Kabbalist tradition.[66] Women served as priests and could administer even the most important rite, the consolamentum.[67] Cathars were closely associated with the Troubadours, the writers of romantic poetry, and were thought to believe that God was manifest in nature's colors and sounds.[68] They were liked and protected both by the upper classes and by their Catholic neighbors to such an extent that, when the Roman Catholic Church later attacked, many Catholics chose to die rather than turn their Catharan neighbors over to the Church.[69]

Responding to the growing popularity of the Cathars, the Catholic Church accused them of the standard malefactions: desecrating the cross and the sacraments, cannibalism, renouncing Christ, and sexual orgies.[70] And, yet, the Catholic St. Bernard, who was hardly a friend of the Cathars, said of them:

> *If you interrogate them, nothing can be more*
> *Christian; as to their conversation, nothing can*
> *be less reprehensible, and what they speak they*
> *prove by deeds. As for the morals of the heretic,*
> *he cheats no one, he oppresses no one, he*

strikes no one; his cheeks are pale with fasting,
he eats not the bread of idleness, his hands
labor for his livelihood.[71]

Circulating scandalous stories of Catharan atrocities did little either to check the Cathars' popularity or to stem the tide of tolerance and independent thought. Disregarding one of the

5.5 - Innocent III, Pope from 1198 to 1216.

Church's most severe sentences, the town of Viterbo even elected an excommunicated heretic as chamberlain.[72]

In 1139 the Church began calling councils to condemn the Cathars and all who supported them.[73] By 1179 Alexander III proclaimed a crusade against these enemies of the Church promising two years' indulgence, or freedom from punishment for sins, to all who would take up arms, and eternal salvation for any who should die. While this set a precedent for providing the Church with a warlike militia to fight the Church's private quarrels,[74] it failed to rally force against the popular Cathars. Then in 1204 Pope Innocent III destroyed what remained of the independence of local churches when he armed his legates with the authority "to destroy, throw down, or pluck up whatever is to be destroyed, thrown down, or plucked up and to plant and build whatever is to be built or planted."[75] In 1208 when Innocent III offered, in addition to indulgences and eternal salvation, the lands and property of the heretics and their supporters to any who would take up arms, the Albigensian Crusade to slaughter the Cathars began.

The savagery of the thirty-year-long attack decimated Langedoc. At the Cathedral of St. Nazair alone 12,000 people were killed. Bishop Folque of Toulouse put to death 10,000.[76] When the crusaders fell upon the town of Beziers and the commanding legate, Arnaud, was asked how to distinguish Catholic from Cathar, he replied, "Kill them all, for God knows his own!"[77] Not a child was spared. One historian wrote that "even the dead were not safe from dishonor, and the worst humiliations were heaped upon women."[78] The total slain at Beziers as reported by papal legates was 20,000, by other chroniclers the numbers killed were between 60,000 and 100,000.[79] The Albigensian crusade killed an estimated one million people, not only Cathars but much of the population of southern France. Afterwards, with its population nearly annihilated, its buildings left in rubble, and its economy destroyed, the lands of southern France were annexed to the north.

Entrenched in its authoritarian structure and consumed by the belief in its own supremacy, the Catholic Church was unable to respond to the rapid growth and changes of medieval society. Instead it demanded obedience to the Pope's dictates. When crusades against the Muslim, Greek and Jewish infidel failed to bring about lasting European unity under the banner of Christianity, the Church struck closer to home, attacking anyone who threatened its power or disobeyed its commands. Its thirty-year-long Albigensian crusade ushered in a five-hundred-year-long period of brutal repression, the length and scope of which has no parallel in the Western world.

ﺐ ﺐ ﺐ

Chapter Six

Controlling
the Human Spirit:
the Inquisition and Slavery

1250 - 1800

There has been no more organized effort by a religion to control people and contain their spirituality than the Christian Inquisition. Developed within the Church's own legal framework, the Inquisition attempted to terrify people into obedience. As the Inquisitor Francisco Pena stated in 1578, "We must remember that the main purpose of the trial and execution is not to save the soul of the accused but to achieve the public good and put fear into others."[1] The Inquisition took countless human lives in Europe and around the world as it followed in the wake of missionaries. And along with the tyranny of the Inquisition, churchmen also brought religious justification for the practice of slavery.

The unsubmissive spirit of the high Middle Ages only seemed to exacerbate the Church's demand for unquestioning obedience. The Church's understanding of God was to be the only understanding. There was to be no discussion or debate. As the Inquisitor Bernard Gui said, the layman must not argue with the unbeliever, but "thrust his sword into the man's belly as far as it will go."[2] In a time of burgeoning ideas about spirituality, the Church insisted that it was the only avenue through which one was permitted to learn of God. Pope Innocent III declared "that anyone who attempted to construe a personal view of God which conflicted with Church dogma must be burned without pity."[3]

Before the Inquisition was fully underway, the Church welcomed heretics back to its fold under terms it considered reasonable. The following is an example of such terms:

> On three Sundays the penitent is to be stripped to the waist and scourged by the priest from the entrance of the town... to the church door. He is to abstain forever from meat and eggs and cheese, except on Easter, Pentecost, and Christmas, when he is to eat of them as sign of his abnegation of his Manichaean errors. For twoscore days, twice a year, he is to forgo the use of fish, and for three days in each week that of fish, wine, and oil, fasting, if his health and labors will permit. He is to wear monastic vestments, with a small cross sewed on each breast. If possible, he is to hear mass daily and on feast-days to attend church at vespers. Seven times a day he is to recite the canonical hours, and, in addition the Paternoster ten times each day and twenty times each night. He is to observe the strictest chastity. Every month he is to show this paper to the priest, who is to watch its observance closely, and this mode of life is to be maintained until the legate shall see fit to alter it, while for infraction of the penance he is to be held as a perjurer and a heretic, and to be segregated from the society of the faithful.[4]

Few heretics returned to the Church of their own accord.

The Church turned to its own canon law to authenticate an agency which could enforce adherence to Church authority. In 1231 Pope Gregory IX established the Inquisition as a separate tribunal, independent of bishops and prelates. Its administrators, the inquisitors, were to be answerable only to the Pope.[5] Its inquisitional law replaced the common law tradition of "innocent until proven guilty" with "guilty until proven innocent."[6] Despite an ostensible trial, inquisitional procedure left no possibility for the suspected to prove his or her innocence; the process resulted in the condemnation of anyone even suspected of heresy.[7] The accused was denied the right of counsel.[8] No particulars were given as to the time or place of the suspected heresies, or to what kind of heresies were suspected. A suspected friendship with a convicted heretic was also a crime, yet no information was given as to which heretic the accused was to have "adored." The names of the accusing witnesses were kept secret.[9] One's only recourse was an appeal to the Pope in Rome which was so futile as to be farcical.[10] The friar Bernard Delicieux declared:

> ...that if St. Peter and St. Paul were accused of 'adoring' heretics and were prosecuted after the fashion of the Inquisition, there would be no defense open for them.[11]

The inquisitor presided over inquisitional procedure as both prosecutor and judge. While he was technically to arrive at his decision after consulting with an assembly of experts of his choosing, this check to his power was soon abandoned.[12] An inquisitor was selected primarily on the basis of his zeal to prosecute heretics.[13] He and his assistants, messengers and spies were allowed to carry arms. And in 1245, the Pope granted him the right to absolve these assistants for any acts of violence.[14] This act rendered the Inquisition, which was already free from

---

6.1 Inquisitors presided both as prosecutor and judge, leaving little possibility for someone accused of heresy to ever be proven innocent.

any secular jurisdiction, unaccountable to even ecclesiastical tribunals.

Inquisitors grew very rich. They received bribes and annual fines from the wealthy who paid to escape accusation.[15] The Inquisition would claim all the money and property of alleged heretics.[16] As there was little chance of the accused being proven innocent, there was no need to wait for conviction to confiscate his or her property.[17] Unlike Roman law that reserved a portion of property for the convicted's nearest heirs, canon and inquisitional law left nothing. Pope Innocent III had explained that God punished children for the sins of their parents. So unless children had come forth spontaneously to denounce their parents, they were left penniless. Inquisitors even accused the dead of heresy, sometimes as much as seventy years after their death. They exhumed and burned the alleged heretic's bones and then confiscated all property from the heirs.[18]

Inquisitors rarely shared the money collected with the episcopal courts, the civil government, or spent it building churches as planned.[19] One historian writes how the inquisitor was often able to "seize everything for himself, not even sending a share to the officials of the Inquisition at Rome."[20] Inquisitors were reluctant to pay for even the cost of feeding their victims, encouraging the families or the community to pay such costs. It was hardly a coincidence that the eagerness of the Inquisition in any given region was proportionate to the opportunities for confiscation.[21]

Ironically, inquisitors were most often chosen from Dominican and Franciscan orders, both of which originally professed vows of poverty. The Church did little to encourage their ideal of poverty. Although it regarded the Franciscan founder, Francis of Assisi, as a saint, the Church persecuted Francis's followers who upheld his ideas of poverty, those known as the Fraticelli, or "Spiritual Franciscans." The Church denounced the Fraticelli as "false and pernicious" and in 1315 excommunicated them.[22]

Pope Martin V ordered their village of Magnalata leveled and every resident slain.[23] The Franciscans who abandoned Francis's teachings, however, were often appointed as inquisitors. While it did not overtly endorse the Inquisition's avarice and corruption, the Church did little to stop it.

The Inquisition had devastating economic impact. Aside from directly seizing the property of successful merchants by accusing them of heresy, inquisitors crippled commerce by holding certain operations suspect. For example, maps and map-makers, so essential to navigating traders and merchants, were held in deep suspicion. Inquisitors believed the printed word to be a channel of heresy and so hampered the communication produced by the fifteenth century invention of the printing press.[24] The mere suspicion of heresy annulled all rights of the suspected individual.[25] When accused, all debts owed by the heretic and any liens which secured those debts became null and void. The historian Henry Charles Lea writes:

> As no man could be certain of the orthodoxy of another, it will be evident how much distrust must have been thrown upon even the commonest transactions of life. The blighting influence of this upon the development of commerce and industry can readily be perceived, coming as it did at a time when the commercial and industrial movement of Europe was beginning to usher in the dawn of modern culture.[26]

While inquisitors themselves prospered, their activity left communities impoverished.

The Inquisition was merciless with its victims. The same man who had been both prosecutor and judge decided upon the sentence. In 1244 the Council of Narbonne ordered that in the sentencing of heretics, no husband should be spared because of his wife, nor wife because of her husband, nor parent because of helpless children, and no sentence should be mitigated because of sickness or old age.[27] Each and every sentence included flagellation.

Of the sentences, pilgrimages were considered the lightest. Yet, undertaken on foot, such penances could take years, during which the penitent's family might perish.[28] Carrying a much greater stigma than pilgrimages was "wearing the crosses," also known as *poena confusibilis* or "humiliating punishment." The penitents were required to wear large saffron-colored crosses on the front and back, which subjected them to public ridicule and hindered every effort of earning a livelihood.[29] A more frequent sentence was perpetual imprisonment, which always entailed a scant diet of bread and water, sometimes meant being kept in chains, and occasionally entailed solitary confinement. The life expectancy in all the prison sentences was very short.[30]

The harshest sentence of burning at the stake was given to those who either failed in their previous penance, relapsed into heresy, or who would not confess to any crime. Although the Church had begun killing heretics in the late fourth century and again in 1022 at Orléan, papal statutes of 1231 now insisted that heretics suffer death by fire.[31] Burning people to death technically avoided spilling a drop of blood. The words of the Gospel of John were understood to sanction burning: "If a man abide not in me, he is cast forth as a branch, and is withered; and men gather them, and cast them into the fire, and they are burned."[32]

The Church distanced itself from the killing by turning heretics over to secular authorities for the actual burning. Such secular authorities, however, were not allowed to decline. When the Senate of Venice in 1521 refused to approve such executions, for example, Pope Leo X wrote that secular officials were:

> *...to intervene no more in this kind of trial, but promptly, without changing or inspecting the sentences made by the ecclesiastical judges, to execute the sentences which they are enjoined to carry out. And if they neglect or refuse, you (the*

Papal legate) are to compel them with the
Church's censure and other appropriate
measures. From this order there is no appeal.[33]
In practice, any secular authorities who refused to cooperate
were excommunicated and subject to the same treatment as
suspected heretics.[34]

By far the cruelest aspect of the inquisitional system was the
means by which confessions were wrought: the torture chamber.
Torture remained a legal option for the Church from 1252 when
it was sanctioned by Pope Innocent IV until 1917 when the new
Codex Juris Canonici was put into effect.[35] Innocent IV
authorized indefinite delays to secure confessions, giving
inquisitors as much time as they wanted to torture the accused.[36]
Although the letter of law forbade repeating torture, inquisitors
easily avoided this rule by simply "continuing" torture, calling
any interval a suspension.[37] In 1262 inquisitors and their
assistants were granted the authority to quietly absolve each other
from the crime of bloodshed.[38] They simply explained that the
tortured had died because the devil broke their necks.

Thus, with license granted by the Pope himself, inquisitors
were free to explore the depths of horror and cruelty. Dressed
as black-robed fiends with black cowls over their heads,
inquisitors extracted confessions from nearly anyone. The
Inquisition invented every conceivable devise to inflict pain by
slowly dismembering and dislocating the body. Many of these
devices were inscribed with the motto "Glory be only to God."[39]
The rack, the hoist and water tortures were the most common.
Victims were rubbed with lard or grease and slowly roasted
alive.[40] Ovens built to kill people, made infamous in twentieth
century Nazi Germany, were first used by the Christian
Inquisition in Eastern Europe.[41] Victims were thrown into a pit
full of snakes and buried alive. One particularly gruesome
torture involved turning a large dish full of mice upside down on
the victim's naked stomach. A fire was then lit on top of the dish

causing the mice to panic and burrow into the stomach.[42] Should
a victim withstand such pain without confessing, he or she would
be burned alive at the stake, often in mass public burnings,
called *auto-da-fé*.[43]

Contemporary writings echo the terror created by the
Inquisition. Juan de Mariana reported in the 1490's that people

> ...were deprived of the liberty to hear and talk
> freely, since in all cities, towns and villages
> there were persons placed to give information of
> what went on. This was considered by some the
> most wretched slavery and equal to death.[44]

A writer in 1538 described life in the Spanish city of Toledo:

> ...preachers do not dare to preach, and those
> who preach do not dare to touch on contentious
> matters, for their lives and honour are in the
> mouths of two ignoramuses, and nobody in this
> life is without his policeman... Bit by bit many
> rich people leave the country for foreign realms,
> in order not to live all their lives in fear and
> trembling every time an officer of the Inquisition
> enters their house; for continual fear is a worse
> death than a sudden demise.[45]

The Inquisition often targeted members of other religions as
severely as it did heretics. The Inquisition now lent its authority
to the long-standing Christian persecution of Jews. Particularly
during the Christian Holy Week of the Passion, Christians
frequently rioted against Jews or refused to sell them food in
hopes of starving them.[46] At the beginning of the thirteenth
century, Pope Innocent III required Jews to wear distinctive
clothing.[47] In 1391 the Archdeacon of Seville launched a "Holy

---

6.2   A mass burning or *auto-da-fé*. As one inquisitor stated, "We must
remember that the main purpose of the trial and execution is not to save the
soul of the accused but to achieve the public good and put fear into
others."[48]

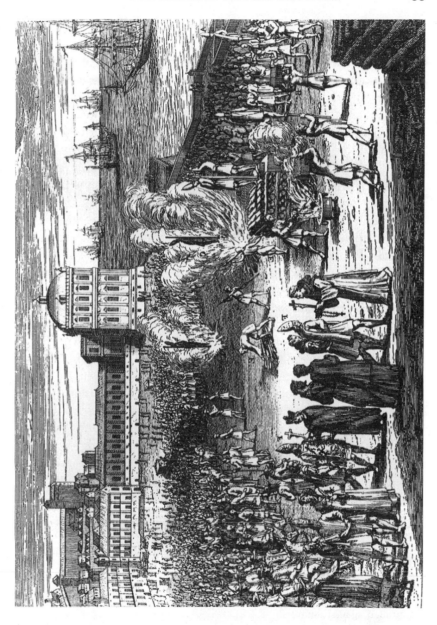

War against the Jews."[49] By 1492 the Inquisition in Spain had become so virulent in its persecution of Jews that it demanded either their conversion to Christianity or their expulsion. Muslims experienced little better. Not surprisingly, Islamic countries offered far safer sanctuaries to escaping Jews than Christian lands.

Historians have often diminished Christian responsibility for the Inquisition by dividing the Inquisition into three separate phases: the medieval, the Spanish and the Roman. The greater secular influence of King Ferdinand and Queen Isabella is thought to separate the Spanish Inquisition from the medieval. Yet, the Spanish Inquisition's most influential leader, the Dominican Tomás de Torquemada, was appointed Inquisitor General by Pope Sixtus IV. Jews were expelled from Spain, not from a profit motive (there was little money to be made in banishing a large community whose taxes were paid directly to the crown), but from the fear that Jews contaminated Christian society.[50] The Roman Inquisition is distinct from the medieval mainly because it was renamed. In 1542 Pope Paul III reassigned the medieval Inquisition to the Congregation of the Inquisition, or the Holy Office. Each phase was identical, however, in its demand for absolute submission of the individual to authority, a demand rooted in the orthodox conviction that God similarly requires unquestioning obedience.

The tyranny inherent in the belief in singular supremacy accompanied explorers and missionaries throughout the world. When Columbus landed in America in 1492, he mistook it for India and called the native inhabitants "Indians." It was his avowed aim to "convert the heathen Indians to our Holy Faith"[51] that warranted the enslaving and exporting of thousands of Native Americans. That such treatment resulted in complete

---

6.3 A painting of Christopher Columbus landing in the New World. His converting native inhabitants to Christianity seemed to justify the atrocities committed against them.

genocide did not matter as much as that these natives had been given the opportunity of everlasting life through their exposure to Christianity.[52] The same sort of thinking also gave Westerners license to rape women. In his own words, Columbus described how he himself "took [his] pleasure" with a native woman after whipping her "soundly" with a piece of rope.[53]

The Inquisition quickly followed in their wake. By 1570 the Inquisition had established an independent tribunal in Peru and the city of Mexico for the purpose of "freeing the land, which has become contaminated by Jews and heretics."[54] Natives who did not convert to Christianity were burned like any other heretic.[55] The Inquisition spread as far as Goa, India, where in the late 16th and early 17th centuries it took no less than 3,800 lives.[56]

Even without the formal Inquisition present, missionary behavior clearly illustrated the belief in the supremacy of a single *image* of God, not in the supremacy of one all-encompassing divinity. If the image of God venerated in a foreign land was not Christian, it was simply not divine. Portuguese missionaries in the Far East destroyed pagodas, forced scholars to hide their religious manuscripts, and suppressed older customs.[57] Mayan scribes in Central America wrote:

> Before the coming of the Spaniards, there was
> no robbery or violence. The Spanish invasion
> was the beginning of tribute, the beginning of
> church dues, the beginning of strife.[58]

In 1614 the Shogun of Japan, Iyeyazu, accused the missionaries of "wanting to change the government of the country and make themselves masters of the soil."[59]

With no understanding of shared supremacy and authority, missionaries fought among themselves just as had early orthodox

---

6.4 Some missionaries felt that it was their right to kill native inhabitants who refused to convert to Christianity or submit to the Church.

Christians who had "wanted to command one another" and lusted "for power over one another."[60] In Japan and China, the Dominicans fought bitterly with the Jesuits. In the Near East, the Franciscans fought with the Capuchins. And in India, the Jesuits fought several wars against the Capuchins.[61] A Seneca chief asked of a Moravian missionary in 1805, "If there is but one religion, why do you white people differ so much about it?"[62]

Missionaries often took part in the unscrupulous exploitation of foreign lands. Many became missionaries to get rich quickly and then return to Europe to live off their gains. In Mexico, Dominicans, Augustinians and Jesuits were known to own "the largest flocks of sheep, the finest sugar ingenios, the best kept estates..."[63] The Church, particularly in South America, supported the enslavement of native inhabitants and the theft of native lands. A 1493 papal Bull justified declaring war on any natives in South America who refused to adhere to Christianity.[64] As the jurist Encisco claimed in 1509:

> The king has every right to send his men to the Indies to demand their territory from these idol-aters because he had received it from the pope. If the Indians refuse, he may quite legally fight them, kill them and enslave them, just as Joshua enslaved the inhabitants of the country of Canaan.[65]

Orthodox Christians defended slavery as part of the divinely ordained hierarchical order. Passages in the Bible support the institution of slavery:

> Both thy bondmen, and thy bondmaids, which thou shalt have, shall be of the heathen that are round about you; of them shall ye buy bondmen and bondmaids. Moreover of the children of the strangers that do sojourn among you, of them shall ye buy, and of their families that are with you, which they begat in your land: and they

shall be your possession. And ye shall take them
as an inheritance for your children after you, to
inherit them for a possession; they shall be your
bondmen for ever.[66]
St. Paul instructed slaves to obey their masters.[67] The early St.
John Chrysostom wrote:
The slave should be resigned to his lot, in obey-
ing his master he is obeying God...[68]
And in the *City of God*, St. Augustine wrote:
...slavery is now penal in character and planned
by that law which commands the preservation of
the natural order and forbids disturbance.[69]
While there were missionaries who recognized the humanity
of Native Americans and worked earnestly to improve their lot,
few recognized an inherent injustice in the idea of slavery. Even
the well-known Jesuit Antonio Vieira, who was imprisoned by
the Inquisition for his work on behalf of the native inhabitants,
advocated importing black Africans to serve as slaves for
colonial settlers. And he still considered fugitives from slavery
guilty of sin and worthy of excommunication.[70]

Orthodox Christianity also supported the practice of slavery
in North America. The eighteenth century Anglican Church
made it clear that Christianity freed people from eternal damnation, not from the bonds of slavery. The Bishop of London,
Edmund Gibson, wrote:
The Freedom which Christianity gives, is a
Freedom from the Bondage of Sin and Satan,
and from the Dominion of Men's Lusts and
Passions and inordinate Desires; but as to their
outward Condition, whatever that was before,
whether bond or free, their being baptised, and
becoming Christians, makes no manner of
Change in it.[71]
Slaves should, however, be converted to Christianity, it was

argued, because they would then become more docile and obedient.[72]

Both the Inquisition and those supporting the practice of slavery relied upon the same religious justification. In keeping with the orthodox Christian belief in a singular and fearful God who rules at the pinnacle of hierarchy, power resided solely with authority, not with the individual. Obedience and submission were valued far more than freedom and self-determination. The Inquisition played out the darkest consequences of such a belief system as it imprisoned and killed the bodies and spirits of countless people—and not simply for a brief moment of time. The Inquisition spanned centuries and was still active in some places as late as 1834.[73]

ào ào ào

Chapter Seven

The Reformation: Converting the Populace

1500 - 1700 C.E.

Both the Protestant Reformation and the Catholic Counter Reformation attempted to purge Christianity of pre-Christian and pagan elements. While the medieval Church had embraced orthodox ideology in theory, in practice it had concerned itself far more with amassing wealth and enforcing social obedience than with directing the spirituality of common people. Reformers now set about teaching the European populace a better understanding of orthodox Christianity. By frightening people with stories of the devil and the danger of magic, they convinced people to believe in an authoritarian God who demanded discipline, struggle, and the renunciation of physical pleasure.

Protesting a Church more concerned with collecting money than with teaching scripture, Martin Luther ignited the Protestant Reformation. When he posted his 95 theses on the door of his town's church in 1517, Luther gave voice to a widespread resentment of the Church. His protest found support among the exploited peasantry, those who advocated independence from the Holy Roman Empire, and those who resented the money being sent to the Church in Rome and the Church's immense landed

estates. Protestantism soon swept through Germany, Switzerland, the Low Countries, England, Scotland, the Scandinavian Kingdoms, as well as through parts of France, Hungary and Poland.

The Catholic Church responded with its own Reformation, called the Counter Reformation, centered around the decisions and canons of the Council of Trent which met between 1545 and 1563. The animosity between Protestants and Catholics sparked a series of civil wars in France and England as well as the bloody Thirty Years War involving Germany, Sweden, France, Denmark, England, the Netherlands, and the Holy Roman Empire represented by the Hapsburgs. That both sides considered themselves Christian did not temper the bloodshed. On August 24, 1572, for example, in what is known as the massacre of St. Bartholomew's Day, 10,000 Protestants were slaughtered in France. Pope Gregory XIII wrote to France's Charles IX, "We rejoice with you that with the help of God you have relieved the world of these wretched heretics."[1]

Yet, both Protestants and Catholics were concerned with establishing a Christianity based upon orthodox ideology. Protestants led this effort by advocating stricter adherence to scripture. Aided by the printing press, the Protestant message demonstrated more uniformity and was less likely to be adapted to older pagan beliefs.[2] The harsher tenets of the Old Testament took on greater prominence. Rather than invoking God's participation as a helpmate in life as many had continued to do, Protestants believed that one should be more concerned with supplication and obedience to God's sovereign will. Jesus should be seen, not as a human being with whom to relate, but as part of almighty God. Some Protestants even denied that Jesus had taken on a biologically human body; his had been a "celestial flesh."[3]

7.1 A depiction of Martin Luther burning the Papal Bull. His protests against the Catholic Church touched off the Protestant Reformation.

7.2 & 7.3 Depictions of the massacre of Protestants in Calabria (left) and the massacre of St. Bartholomew's Day (above). The presence of two major branches of Christianity, each convinced that theirs was the only true path to God, turned Europe into a bloodbath.

Protestants viewed the worship of saints and Mary, which had an intensely personal tone, as a form of idolatry and a diminishment of Jesus's single-handed victory. An individual, they believed, should develop a relationship with God strictly through the word of scripture rather than through the humanized images of Jesus, Mary, the saints, or even through symbols. Much in the way that fourth century Christians vandalized the sacred sites and images of more ancient traditions, so now Protestant mobs, incited by preachers and with the endorsement of public authority, destroyed images of saints.[4] Although Protestantism vehemently denied the necessity of the Church as an intermediary between the individual and God, it removed most of the means through which a direct and personal relationship might develop.

Catholic reformers also diminished the veneration of saints. Saints were now to be seen as heroic figures and models of virtue rather than as friends or benefactors.[5] But the Catholic Church was reluctant to part with the authority it had built over centuries. Yes, Christian faith should be sourced in the Bible, but—as the Council of Trent declared—the Bible was best clarified by "the testimonies of approved holy fathers and councils, the judgement and consensus of the Church."[6] Catholics were also unwilling to dispense with the ritualistic and sacramental nature of church services. Some Protestants, on the other hand, rejected rituals and sacraments entirely, insisting that one should experience God strictly through preaching or reading scripture.[7]

Protestant leaders fervently embraced St. Augustine's ideas about free will and predestination: that Adam's fall from grace had left humanity inherently flawed, incapable of acting correctly, and thus entirely dependent upon God's mercy. Salvation was now possible only through the grace of God, not through individual determination. "Free will after the Fall is nothing but a word," said Luther in 1518. "Even doing what in him lies, man sins mortally."[8] Most Catholics believed that while Adam's sin had inclined us towards evil and diminished our free will, his sin had not destroyed our free will entirely. Canon Four of the Council of Trent reads:

If anyone says that man's free will, moved and stimulated by God, cannot cooperate at all by giving its assent to God when he stimulates and calls him... and that he cannot dissent, if he so wills, but like an inanimate creature is utterly inert and passive, let him be anathema.[9]

Even though Protestants lacked the organized Catholic hierarchy to demarcate who was better than whom, they continued to rank human beings. Martin Luther believed that differences in gender, class, race, and belief indicated superior and inferior states of being. In 1533 he wrote, "Girls begin to talk and to stand on their feet sooner than boys because weeds always grow up more quickly than good crops."[10] In 1525 he supported the merciless suppression of the Peasants' War, a rebellion that his own spirit of independence from the Roman Church had helped to ignite.[11] Although Luther could find no scriptural warrant for exterminating Jews, he believed that they should be enslaved or thrown out of Christian lands and that their ghettos and synagogues should be burned.[12] He thought that the rebellious Anabaptists should be killed and even publicly affirmed a 1531 edict by Wittenberg theologians sanctioning their execution.[13]

Other Protestant leaders were no more tolerant. John Calvin, whose doctrine formed the basis of Presbyterianism, wrote of:

...the eternal principle, by which [God] has determined what He will do with each man. For He does not create them equal, but appoints some to eternal life, and others to eternal damnation.[14]

Calvin established a powerfully repressive, police-state theocracy in Geneva that is perhaps best remembered for burning the well-known physician, Michael Servetus, because of his dissenting views of Christianity. Calvin's pupil, John Knox, condemned all other creeds. As Protestants fragmented, each new denomination laid claim to the sole divine truth, denouncing all others.

In keeping with their belief in an authoritarian God, both Protestants and Catholics advocated strict enforcement of their perception of God's laws. The Catholic Church had already established the means with which to control society and enforce obedience. Protestants, however, lacked the well-developed judicial structure and hierarchy of the Catholic Church and lacked its global reach. Instead, they transferred the enforcement of personal morality to the state. Aside from its secular functions, the state should now uphold the moral purity of society; it should be "the Godly state."[15]   The domestic family unit, governed by the father, also took on new importance as the microcosm of the authoritarian structure.

Both Protestants and Catholics diminished the important role of the community, making it easier for the Church and state to have more direct control of the individual. The Reformation discouraged fraternities, which in the Middle Ages had provided for its members in times of need, organized celebrations and plays, helped care for the poor, and set up hospitals.[16] Community festivals, crucial to the harmony and vitality of the community, were curtailed. Catholic confessions, which had been a public act of forgiveness that restored a sinner back into the community, became a private matter between the individual and the priest with the introduction of the confession-box in 1565.[17] And the role of god-parents, which had served to cement social ties in ritual friendship, was diminished.[18] The Reformation eroded the community's capacity to intervene with the authority of the Church, state, or family patriarch.

The Reformation—both Protestant and Catholic—replaced the importance of communal harmony with an emphasis upon Godly order and obedience. The ten commandments took the place of the doctrine of the seven deadly sins which had formed the core of medieval morality: pride, envy, anger, avarice, gluttony, sloth and lechery. Those sins that destroyed the sense of community had been considered the worst: pride, envy, anger and avarice. The most important of the ten commandments, however, was the one that upheld, not communal harmony, but parental and civil authority: "Honour thy father and mother."[19] Some laws in Puritan New England even decreed the death penalty for young who might curse or "smite" their parents.[20] Sin, rather than something which disrupted communal harmony, now came to be seen as disobedience to authority.[21]

Reformers had become aware not only of how little respect the Church commanded, but also of how ignorant common people were of orthodox Christianity. In 1547 Stephen Gardner described a parish in Cambridge: "when the vicar goeth into the pulpit to read that [he] himself hath written, then the multitude of the parish goeth straight out of the church, home to drink."[22] The historian Keith Thomas reports how, when a rector in Essex "preached in 1630 about Adam and Eve making themselves coats of fig-leaves, one loud-mouthed parishioner demanded to know where they got the thread to sew them with."[23] Orthodox Christianity was especially foreign to people in rural areas. In 1607 John Norden wrote:

> In some parts where I have travelled, where
> great and spacious wastes, mountains and heaths
> are, ...many cottages are set up, the people
> given to little or no kind of labour, living very
> hardly with oaten bread, sour whey, and goat's
> milk, dwelling far from any church or chapel,
> and are as ignorant of God or of any course of
> life as the very savages amongst the infidels.[24]

To deal with the paganism of common people, Protestants and Catholics during the Reformation focused upon teaching the concept of a singular, heavenly God. In contrast to their understanding of divinity through a multiplicity of faces that could be experienced in every aspect of life, people were now taught to understand God strictly as a heavenly father who was no longer part of or interested in the physical realm. Spirituality, or a relationship with God, lay in repudiating physical pleasure, which often encompassed not just the pleasure of the physical senses but simple comforts as well. The late seventeenth century Tronson went so far as to declare:

> *If you want to be heirs of Jesus and paradise,*
> *that is, if you want not to be damned everlast-*
> *ingly but to be happy for ever in heaven, then*
> *you must renounce the world entirely and bid it*
> *an eternal farewell.*[25]

The physical body was also to be repudiated. Since God was no longer to be found in the physical, the body was ungodly. Protestants and Catholics competed with each other over how little they could care for their bodies, using little soap and water throughout a lifetime.[26] A Jesuit in the 1700's, explaining that "religious modesty" is enough to prevent anyone from bathing, told a story of one who violated the prohibition:

> *A youth who dared to bathe at one of our coun-*
> *try houses did drown there, perhaps by God's*
> *merciful judgement, for He may have wished this*
> *fearful example to serve as law.*[27]

A Catholic sermon from around 1700 advises one "to treat one's body as a sworn enemy, and subdue it through work, fasts, hairshirts, and other mortifications."[28] A Sorbonne prior and doctor named Joseph Lambert warned rural folk:

> *...you must regard every kind of touching of*
> *your own and others' bodies, every liberty, as*
> *the most serious of sins; although these lewd acts*
> *may indeed be secret, they are loathsome in*
> *God's sight, who sees them all, is offended by*
> *them, and never fails to punish them most*
> *severely.*[29]

While orthodox Christians had long considered sex for any purpose other than procreation to be sinful, it was only during the Reformation that most common people learned this. Christian history is replete with condemnations of human sexuality. In the fifth century St. Augustine developed a theory not only of how sin passed from generation to generation by the sexual act, but also how sexual desire was in itself proof of the lack of human free will. Inquisitors at the turn of the sixteenth century wrote that "God allows the devil more power over the venereal act, by which the original sin is handed down, than over other human actions."[30] Reformers now took such attitudes and exhorted ordinary people to repudiate sexual pleasure even within a heterosexual marriage. It became common, for example, to cite Jerome's remark that a husband committed a sin if he enjoyed sex with his wife too much.[31]

Pleasure in any form was now to be repudiated. Grignon de Montfort, a Catholic missionary, denounced love songs, tales and romances "which spread like the plague... and corrupt so many people."[32] A prominent eighteenth century Augustinian priest repeatedly condemned public entertainment. "Public performances are inherently opposed to the spirit of Christianity." "Plays give only dangerous lessons." "Plays are the source of our time's dissoluteness."[33] In seventeenth century New England where Puritans controlled much of society, warnings or actual punishment befell any youths caught sledding or swimming and any adults caught simply enjoying themselves when they might be better employed.[34] To enjoy oneself on the Sabbath was considered a terrible offense. A Massachusetts law of 1653 prohibited Sunday walks and visits to the harbor as being a waste of time. Playing children or strolling young men and women were warned that they were engaging in "things tending much to the dishonor of God, the reproach of religion and the prophanation of the holy Sabbath."[35] John Lewis and

Sarah Chapman were brought before the New London court in 1670 for "sitting together on the Lord's Day, under an apple tree in Goodman Chapman's orchard."[36]

The pleasures of physical beauty and aesthetics were similarly disparaged. The seventeenth century bastion of Puritanism in New England frowned upon ornamentation of any sort. Furniture and dwellings were extremely austere. Beautiful clothing was considered sinful. In 1634 the General Court forbade garments:

> ...with any lace on it, silver, gold or thread...
> also all cutworks, embroidered or needlework
> caps, bands and rails... all gold and silver
> girdles, hatbands, belts, ruffs, beaver hats.[37]

Clothing which revealed the female body was illegal. A 1650 New England law prohibited "short sleeves, whereby the nakedness of the arm may be discovered."[38] Christians came to believe that anything which focused attention upon the physical world was ungodly.

The perceived separation of humanity from a strictly heavenly God produced a great sense of shame during the Reformation. Ignatius of Loyola, the founder of the Jesuits, declared:

> I am mere dung, I must ask our Lord that when
> I am dead my body be thrown on the dungheap
> to be devoured by the birds and dogs... Must
> this not be my wish in punishment for my sins?[39]

And Calvin wrote:

> We are all made of mud, and this mud is not just
> on the hem of our gown, or on the sole of our
> boots, or in our shoes. We are full of it, we are
> nothing but mud and filth both inside and out-
> side.[40]

7.4   John Knox, the founder of Scottish Presbyterianism. Believing the physical world to be ungodly, Protestant reformers condemned pleasure of any sort: physical, sexual or aesthetic.

In the mid-1700's Jonathan Edwards, the Calvinist New England theologian, preached:

(You are) a little, wretched, despicable creature;
a worm, a mere nothing, and less than nothing;
a vile insect, that has risen up in contempt
against the majesty of heaven and earth.[41]

One should cope with one's intrinsically evil nature through discipline, chastisement and struggle. Reformers extolled discipline and struggle as measures of a person's spirituality and godliness. Much of the Catholic Counter Reformation focused upon the administration and education of priests so that they could better teach discipline and the laws of the almighty God to their parishioners. Penance became a means of avoiding sinful behavior rather than a way of making amends for sins already committed.[42] The Puritan Cotton Mather affirmed the value of punishment and echoed Augustine's "compel them to enter" with his famous phrase "Better whipt, than Damn'd."[43]

Suffering and hardship marked a true orthodox Christian's life. Jesus's greatest act was understood to be, not his miracles of healing or his courageous rebellion against injustice, but his suffering and dying on the cross. The Church canonized individuals as saints, not because of their ease of accomplishment, but because of their torment and martyrdom. As the poet of the *Spiritual Canticle* wrote, one may not "look for Christ without the cross," and "suffering is the livery of those who love..."[44] The seventeenth century Antoine Godeau preached that "a true Christian takes joy in having some afflictions to suffer, because suffering is the badge of a true Christian."[45]

Magic, or the belief that God could intervene and make physical life easier, became a sure sign of ungodliness during the Reformation. God reigned from above and demanded hard work and suffering. As the historian Keith Thomas notes, "man was to earn his bread by the sweat of his brow."[46] Magic was also perceived as an arrogant attempt to impersonate God. For, as one reformer asked in 1554, "if ye may make at your pleasure such things to drive devils away and to deal both body and soul, what need have ye of Christ?"[47]   According to the seventeenth century Francis Bacon, magical remedies should be shunned because they "propound those noble effects which God hath set forth unto man to be bought at the price of labour, to be attained by a few easy and slothful observances."[48]   John Cotta, an English physician of the same period, wrote:

> God hath given nothing unto man but for his travail and pain; and according to his studious industry, care, prudence, providence, assiduity and diligence, he dispenseth unto him every good thing. He hath not ordained wonders and miracles to give supply unto our common needs, nor to answer the ordinary occasions or uses of our life.[49]

This was news to much of medieval Europe. Most people still believed in a multifaceted God who could be called upon to assist in everyday life. The early Church, unable to convert people from such a belief, had established its own system of ecclesiastical magic.[50] The Church had a whole range of formulas involving prayer and the invocation of God's name designed to encourage God's assistance in practical, secular matters. So strong was the belief in the power of the spoken word, for instance, that the Church discouraged people from learning exactly what the priest was saying for fear that they would be able to use such powerful words to work their own magic.[51] And so strong was the belief that perjury would summon God's vengeance, that the Church relied upon a witness's honesty in testifying after he or she had sworn an oath upon a Bible or a relic.[52] The belief in the magical power of the word was still so prevalent in Protestant England that in 1624 the Parliament passed an act prohibiting swearing and cursing.[53]

It was against the medieval Church's endorsement of magic

that Protestants most fervently rebelled. "The Papists," wrote Calvin, "pretend there is a magical force in the sacraments, independent of efficacious faith..."[54]   The Calvinist James Calfhill proclaimed that "the vilest witches and sorcerers of the earth" were

>...the priests that consecrate crosses and ashes,
>water and salt, oil and cream, boughs and
>bones, stocks and stones; that christen bells that
>hang in the steeple; that conjure worms that
>creep in the field; that give St. John's Gospel to
>hang about men's necks...[55]

Protestants attacked sacraments such as confirmation as nothing

>...but plain sorcery, devilry, witchcraft, jug-
>gling, legerdemain, and all that naught is. The
>bishop mumbleth a few Latin words over the
>child, charmeth him, crosseth him, smeareth him
>with stinking popish oil, and tieth a linen brand
>about the child's neck and sendeth him home...[56]

"The sacraments," wrote John Canne in 1634, "were not ordained by God to be used... as charms and sorceries."[57]

Magic not only attested to what reformers believed was a false understanding of God, it also interfered with the new method of indicating social rank. Pre-reformational society had designated a man's rank either by his position within the Church hierarchy or by his status as a noble or fighter. But as the Church hierarchy and the role of nobility declined, financial

---

7.5 This caricature of the Pope mocked the sacramental nature of the Catholic Church and was popular among Protestants in England, Holland and Germany for over a century.   Articles used in Catholic worship compose the figure: the hat is a church-bell decorated with holy-water brushes, the mouth an open wine flagon, the eye a chalice covered by the holy wafer, the cheek a plate used in the communion service, the shoulder the mass-book.

success became one of the only means of identifying a person's position in the divine hierarchy. Wealth was considered to be a symbol of a person's hard work and spiritual evolution. Such a "Puritan work ethic" would crumble, however, if a person could achieve prosperity magically.

The increased significance of financial success did not, however, lead churchmen to encourage poor people to escape their poverty or to better their lot. The poor were to endure financial injustice without protest. A seventeenth century preacher explained that:

> *If there are people who abuse the authority of sovereigns and charge you unfair taxes, God allows it in order to enact His justice, to punish your sins and the ill use you make of your property.*[58]

A missionary hymn from the eighteenth century called *An exhortation for working people* urges people to bear their station in life quietly:

> *Do not suffer to complain*
> *Of life's arduous pain,*
> *And harbor no envy*
> *For those who dwell on high.*[59]

To believe that you could change your situation through any means other than hard work and struggle, to believe in divine assistance, indicated collusion with the devil. Reformers taught that God was in heaven, not on earth. Any supernatural energy in the physical world could therefore only be the work of the devil and his demons. Indeed, the whole belief in and fear of the devil became paramount during the Reformation. Martin Luther reported having physical encounters with the devil and

---

7.6   Reformers taught that God no longer took part in the physical world; the world was now the realm of only the devil and his demons, such as the one depicted in this woodcut. Anything magical or supernatural could now only be the devil's work.

wrote, "We are all subject to the Devil, both in body and goods..."[60] According to Luther, "The Devil liveth, yea, and reigneth throughout the whole world..."[61] Jean Calvin said that the true Christian saint had to engage in an "unceasing struggle against him"[62] and John Knox called the devil the "prince and God of this world."[63] The Trent Catechism echoed the importance of belief in the devil:

> *Many imagine that the whole matter is fictitious, since they think that they are not attacked themselves. This means that they are in the power of the Devil and have no Christian virtue. Therefore the Devil has no need to tempt them, as their souls are already the Devil's abode.*[64]

Belief in the devil's power became an essential counterpart to the belief in God. The Protestant Roger Hutchinson wrote:

> *If there be a God, as we most steadfastly must believe, verily there is a Devil also; and if there be a Devil, there is no surer argument, no stronger proof, no plainer evidence, that there is a God.*[65]

Another writer pointed out that "he that can already believe that there is no Devil will ere long believe that there is no God..."[66] Like the early Mannichaeans, reformed Christians emphasized belief in the devil as much if not more than belief in God. The catechism of the Jesuit Canisius, for example, mentions the name of satan more often than it does the name of Jesus.[67]

The perceived power of satan increased proportionately with the spread of orthodox Christianity. Belief in the devil is a means of frightening people into obedience. Churchmen of the Reformation were no different from earlier orthodox Christians who had considered fear to be imperative. In 1674 Christophe Schrader advised other preachers of the necessity of having:

> *...a very great fear of the all-powerful and excellent God who chased the rebel angels from*

heaven and our first ancestors from paradise, destroyed practically the whole universe with the deluge, and overthrew whole kingdoms and cities.[68]

The devil is a necessary counterpart to such an "all-powerful and excellent" God. The devil carries out God's judgment, tormenting sinners for all eternity. He is, as King James I called him, "God's hangman."[69]

Like many orthodox doctrines and ideas, belief in the devil makes people feel powerless. Attributing malevolence and negativity to the devil removes responsibility from human beings—as well as the power that accompanies responsibility. For, if one is responsible for something, one can do something about it. But if negativity comes from an external devil, one can do little but cower in fear or attack those who represent the devil. Like the belief in the lack of human free will, the belief in the devil engenders a sense of powerlessness, making people easier to control.

The Reformation brought profound and dramatic change. Nations and imperial powers claimed their independence from the Pope. Medieval social structures and values changed. Perhaps most significantly, the Reformation changed the way people perceived the world. The physical world, once a divine, magical creation, was now understood to be alien to God, belonging only to the devil. The spiritual path was to be marked by suffering, struggle and chastisement. Together the Protestant Reformation and Catholic Counter Reformation converted the people of Europe to orthodox Christianity.

ૐ. ૐ. ૐ.

Chapter Eight

The Witch Hunts:
The End of Magic
and Miracles

1450 - 1750 C.E.

The Reformation did not convert the people of Europe to orthodox Christianity through preaching and catechisms alone. It was the 300 year period of witch-hunting from the fifteenth to the eighteenth century, what R.H. Robbins called "the shocking nightmare, the foulest crime and deepest shame of western civilization,"[1] that ensured the European abandonment of the belief in magic. The Church created the elaborate concept of devil worship and then, used the persecution of it to wipe out dissent, subordinate the individual to authoritarian control, and openly denigrate women.

The witch hunts were an eruption of orthodox Christianity's vilification of women, "the weaker vessel," in St. Peter's words.[2] The second century St. Clement of Alexandria wrote: "Every woman should be filled with shame by the thought that she is a woman."[3] The Church father Tertullian explained why women deserve their status as despised and inferior human beings:

*And do you not know that you are an Eve? The
sentence of God on this sex of yours lives in this
age: the guilt must of necessity live too. You are
the devil's gateway: you are the unsealer of that
tree: you are the first deserter of the divine law:
you are she who persuaded him whom the devil
was not valiant enough to attack. You destroyed
so easily God's image, man. On account of your
desert—that is, death—even the Son of God had
to die.*[4]

Others expressed the view more bluntly. The sixth century
Christian philosopher, Boethius, wrote in *The Consolation of
Philosophy*, "Woman is a temple built upon a sewer."[5] Bishops
at the sixth century Council of Mâcon voted as to whether
women had souls.[6] In the tenth century Odo of Cluny declared,
"To embrace a woman is to embrace a sack of manure..."[7] The
thirteenth century St. Thomas Aquinas suggested that God had
made a mistake in creating woman: "nothing [deficient] or
defective should have been produced in the first establishment of
things; so woman ought not to have been produced then."[8] And
Lutherans at Wittenberg debated whether women were really
human beings at all.[9] Orthodox Christians held women responsible for all sin. As the Bible's Apocrypha states, "Of woman
came the beginning of sin/ And thanks to her, we all must
die."[10]

Women are often understood to be impediments to spirituality
in a context where God reigns strictly from heaven and demands
a renunciation of physical pleasure. As I Corinthians 7:1 states,
"It is a good thing for a man to have nothing to do with a
woman." The Inquisitors who wrote the *Malleus Maleficarum*,
"The Hammer of the Witches," explained that women are more
likely to become witches than men:

*'Because the female sex is more concerned with
things of the flesh than men;' because being*

formed from a man's rib, they are 'only imper-
fect animals' and 'crooked' whereas man be-
longs to a privileged sex from whose midst
Christ emerged.[11]

King James I estimated that the ratio of women to men who
"succumbed" to witchcraft was twenty to one.[12] Of those
formally persecuted for witchcraft, between 80 to 90 percent
were women.[13]

Christians found fault with women on all sorts of counts. An
historian notes that thirteenth century preachers

...denounced women on the one hand for... the
'lascivious and carnal provocation' of their
garments, and on the other hand for being over-
industrious, too occupied with children and
housekeeping, too earthbound to give due
thought to divine things.[14]

According to a Dominican of the same period, woman is "the
confusion of man, an insatiable beast, a continuous anxiety, an
incessant warfare, a daily ruin, a house of tempest ...a hindrance
to devotion."[15]

As reformational fervor spread, the feminine aspect of
Christianity in the worship of Mary became suspect. Throughout
the Middle Ages, Mary's powers were believed to effectively
curtail those of the devil.[16] But Protestants entirely dismissed
reverence for Mary while reformed Catholics diminished her
importance. Devotion to Mary often became indicative of evil.
In the Canary islands, Aldonca de Vargas was reported to the
Inquisition after she smiled at hearing mention of the Virgin
Mary.[17] Inquisitors distorted an image of the Virgin Mary into
a device of torture, covering the front side of a statue of Mary
with sharp knives and nails. Levers would move the arms of the
statue crushing the victim against the knives and nails.[18]

The witch hunts also demonstrated great fear of female
sexuality. The book that served as the manual for understanding

and persecuting witchcraft, the *Malleus Maleficarum*, describes how witches were known to "collect male organs in great numbers, as many as twenty or thirty members together, and put them in a bird's nest..."[19] The manual recounts a story of a man who, having lost his penis, went to a witch to have it restored:

She told the afflicted man to climb a certain
tree, and that he might take which he liked out
of a nest in which there were several members.
And when he tried to take a big one, the witch
said: You must not take that one; adding, be-
cause it belonged to a parish priest.[20]

A man in 1621 lamented, "of women's unnatural, unsatiable lust... what country, what village doth not complain."[21]

While most of what became known as witchcraft was invented by Christians, certain elements of witchcraft did represent an older pagan tradition. Witchcraft was linked and even considered to be synonymous with "divination," which means not only the art of foretelling the future, but also the discovery of knowledge by the aid of supernatural power.[22] It suggests that there is such power available—something orthodox Christians insisted could only be the power of the devil, for God was no longer to be involved with the physical world.

The word "witch" comes from the old English wicce and wicca, meaning the male and female participants in the ancient pagan tradition which holds masculine, feminine and earthly aspects of God in great reverence. Rather than a God which stood above the world, removed from ordinary life, divinity in the Wiccan tradition was understood to imbue both heaven *and* earth. This tradition also recalled a period when human society functioned without hierarchy—either matriarchal or patriarchal— and without gender, racial or strict class rankings. It was a tradition that affirmed the potential for humanity to live without domination and fear, something orthodox Christians maintain is impossible.*

The early Church had tried to eradicate the vestiges of this older non-hierarchical tradition by denying the existence of witches or magic outside of the Church. The *Canon Episcopi*, a Church law which first appeared in 906, decreed that *belief* in witchcraft was heretical.[23] After describing pagan rituals which involved women demonstrating extraordinary powers, it declared:

> *For an innumerable multitude, deceived by this false opinion, believe this to be true and, so believing, wander from the right faith and are involved in the error of the pagans when they think that there is anything of divinity or power except the one God.*[24]

Nevertheless, the belief in magic was still so prevalent in the fourteenth century that the Council of Chartres ordered anathema to be pronounced against sorcerers each Sunday in every church.[25]

It took the Church a long time to persuade society that women were inclined toward evil witchcraft and devil-worship. Reversing its policy of denying the existence of witches, in the thirteenth century the Church began depicting the witch as a slave of the devil.[26] No longer was she or he to be associated with an older pagan tradition. No longer was the witch to be thought of as benevolent healer, teacher, wise woman, or one who accessed divine power. She was now to be an evil satanic agent. The Church began authorizing frightening portrayals of

---

* The idea that humanity could live without domination and violence, far from being an idealistic myth, is beginning to be substantiated by a new picture of human history. The work of James Mellaart, Marija Gimbutas, and Riane Eisler illustrates that humanity lived as much as 25,000 years in peace, much longer than the 3500-5000 years that it has lived with warfare and domination.

the devil in the twelfth and thirteenth centuries.[27] Images of a witch riding a broom first appeared in 1280.[28] Thirteenth century art also depicted the devil's pact in which demons would steal children and in which parents themselves would deliver their children to the devil.[29] The Church now portrayed witches with the same images so frequently used to characterize heretics: "...a small clandestine society engaged in anti-human practices, including infanticide, incest, cannibalism, bestiality and orgiastic sex..."[30]

The Church developed the concept of devil-worship as an astoundingly simplistic reversal of Christian rites and practices. Whereas God imposed divine law, the devil demanded adherence to a pact. Where Christians showed reverence to God by kneeling, witches paid homage to the devil by standing on their heads. The sacraments in the Catholic Church became excrements in the devil's church. Communion was parodied by the Black Mass.[31] Christian prayers could be used to work evil by being recited backwards.[32] The eucharist bread or host was imitated in the devil's service by a turnip. The baptismal "character" or stigmata of the mysteries was parodied by the devil's mark impressed upon the witch's body by the claw of the devil's left hand.[33] Whereas saints had the gift of tears, witches were said to be incapable of shedding tears.[34] Devil worship was a simple parody of Christianity. Indeed, the very concept of the devil was exclusive to monotheism and had no importance within the pagan, Wiccan tradition.

The Church also projected its own hierarchical framework onto this new evil witchcraft. The devil's church was to be organized such that its dignitaries could climb the ranks to the position of bishop, just like in the Catholic Church.[35] Julio Caro Baroja explains:

> ...the Devil causes churches and altars to appear
> with music... and devils decked out as saints.
> The dignitaries reach rank of bishop, and sub-

deacons, deacons and priests serve Mass. Can-
dles and incense are used for the service and
water is sprinkled from a thurifer. There is an
offertory, a sermon, a blessing over the equiva-
lents of bread and wine... So that nothing should
be missing there are even false martyrs in the
organization.[36]

Again, such hierarchy was entirely a projection of the Church
that bore no resemblance to ancient paganism. By recognizing
both masculine and feminine faces of God and by understanding
God to be infused throughout the physical world, the Wiccan
tradition had no need for strict hierarchical rankings.

Pope John XXII formalized the persecution of witchcraft in
1320 when he authorized the Inquisition to prosecute sorcery.[37]
Thereafter papal bulls and declarations grew increasingly
vehement in their condemnation of witchcraft and of all those
who "made a pact with hell."[38] In 1484 Pope Innocent VIII
issued the bull *Summis desiderantes* authorizing two inquisitors,
Kramer and Sprenger, to systematize the persecution of
witches.[39] Two years later their manual, *Malleus Maleficarum*,
was published with 14 editions following between 1487-1520 and
at least 16 editions between 1574-1669.[40] A papal bull in 1488
called upon the nations of Europe to rescue the Church of Christ
which was "imperiled by the arts of Satan."[41] The papacy and
the Inquisition had successfully transformed the witch from a
phenomenon whose existence the Church had previously
rigorously denied into a phenomenon that was deemed very real,
very frightening, the antithesis of Christianity, and absolutely
deserving of persecution.

It was now heresy *not* to believe in the existence of witches.

8.1 A fifteenth century woodcut entitled "Witches Sabbath." Such
characterizations of witchcraft were simplistic reversals of Christian rites
and rituals created by churchmen that had very little to do with the pre-
Christian Wiccan tradition.

As the authors of the *Malleus Maleficarum* noted, "A belief that there are such things as witches is so essential a part of Catholic faith that obstinately to maintain the opposite opinion savors of heresy."[42] Passages in the Bible such as "Thou shalt not suffer a witch to live" were cited to justify the persecution of witches.[43] Both Calvin and Knox believed that to deny witchcraft was to deny the authority of the Bible.[44] The eighteenth century founder of Methodism, John Wesley, declared to those skeptical of witchcraft, "The giving up of witchcraft is in effect the giving up of the Bible."[45] And an eminent English lawyer wrote, "To deny the possibility, nay, actual existence of Witchcraft and Sorcery, is at once flatly to contradict the revealed Word of God in various passages both of the Old and New Testament."[46]

The persecution of witchcraft enabled the Church to prolong the profitability of the Inquisition. The Inquisition had left regions so economically destitute that the inquisitor Eymeric complained, "In our days there are no more rich heretics... it is a pity that so salutary an institution as ours should be so uncertain of its future."[47] By adding witchcraft to the crimes it persecuted, however, the Inquisition exposed a whole new group of people from whom to collect money. It took every advantage of this opportunity. The author Barbara Walker notes:

> *Victims were charged for the very ropes that bound them and the wood that burned them. Each procedure of torture carried its fee. After the execution of a wealthy witch, officials usually treated themselves to a banquet at the expense of the victim's estate.*[48]

In 1592 Father Cornelius Loos wrote:

> *Wretched creatures are compelled by the severity of the torture to confess things they have never done... and so by the cruel butchery innocent lives are taken; and, by a new alchemy, gold and silver are coined from human blood.*[49]

In many parts of Europe trials for witchcraft began exactly as the trials for other types of heresy stopped.[50]

The process of formally persecuting witches followed the harshest inquisitional procedure. Once accused of witchcraft, it was virtually impossible to escape conviction. After cross-examination, the victim's body was examined for the witch's mark. The historian Walter Nigg described the process:

>...*she was stripped naked and the executioner shaved off all her body hair in order to seek in the hidden places of the body the sign which the devil imprinted on his cohorts. Warts, freckles, and birthmarks were considered certain tokens of amorous relations with Satan.*[51]

Should a woman show no sign of a witch's mark, guilt could still be established by methods such as sticking needles in the accused's eyes. In such a case, guilt was confirmed if the inquisitor could find an insensitive spot during the process.[52]

Confession was then extracted by the hideous methods of torture already developed during earlier phases of the Inquisition. "Loathe they are to confess without torture," wrote King James I in his *Daemonologie*.[53] A physician serving in witch prisons spoke of women driven half mad:

>...*by frequent torture... kept in prolonged squalor and darkness of their dungeons... and constantly dragged out to undergo atrocious torment until they would gladly exchange at any moment this most bitter existence for death, are willing to confess whatever crimes are suggested to them rather than to be thrust back into their hideous dungeon amid ever recurring torture.*[54]

Unless the witch died during torture, she was taken to the stake. Since many of the burnings took place in public squares, inquisitors prevented the victims from talking to the crowds by using wooden gags or cutting their tongue out.[55] Unlike a heretic or a Jew who would usually be burnt alive only after they had relapsed into their heresy or Judaism, a witch would be burnt upon the first conviction.[56]

Sexual mutilation of accused witches was not uncommon. With the orthodox understanding that divinity had little or nothing to do with the physical world, sexual desire was perceived to be ungodly. When the men persecuting the accused witches found themselves sexually aroused, they assumed that such desire emanated, not from themselves, but from the woman. They attacked breasts and genitals with pincers, pliers and red-hot irons. Some rules condoned sexual abuse by allowing men deemed "zealous Catholics" to visit female prisoners in solitary confinement while never allowing female visitors. The people of Toulouse were so convinced that the inquisitor Foulques de Saint-George arraigned women for no other reason than to sexually abuse them that they took the dangerous and unusual step of gathering evidence against him.[57]

The horror of the witch hunts knew no bounds. The Church had never treated the children of persecuted parents with compassion, but its treatment of witches' children was particularly brutal. Children were liable to be prosecuted and tortured for witchcraft: girls, once they were nine and a half, and boys, once they were ten and a half.[58] Younger children were tortured in order to elicit testimony that could be used against their parents.[59] Even the testimony of two-year-old children was considered valid in cases of witchcraft though such testimony was never admissible in other types of trials.[60] A famous French magistrate was known to have regretted his leniency when, instead of having young children accused of witchcraft burned, he had only sentenced them to be flogged while they watched their parents burn.[61]

8.2 The torture inflicted upon women accused of witchcraft was especially cruel.

Witches were held accountable for nearly every problem. Any threat to social uniformity, any questioning of authority, and any act of rebellion could now be attributed to and prosecuted as witchcraft. Not surprisingly, areas of political turmoil and religious strife experienced the most intense witch hunts. Witch-hunting tended to be much more severe in Germany, Switzerland, France, Poland and Scotland than in more homogeneously Catholic countries such as Italy and Spain.[62] Witch-hunters declared that "Rebellion is as the sin of Witchcraft."[63] In 1661 Scottish royalists proclaimed that "Rebellion is the mother of witchcraft."[64] And in England the Puritan William Perkins called the witch "The most notorious traytor and rebell that can be..."[65]

The Reformation played a critical role in convincing people to blame witches for their problems. Protestants and reformed Catholics taught that any magic was sinful since it indicated a belief in divine assistance in the physical world. The only supernatural energy in the physical world was to be of the devil. Without magic to counter evil or misfortune, people were left with no form of protection other than to kill the devil's agent, the witch. Particularly in Protestant countries, where protective rituals such as crossing oneself, sprinkling holy water or calling on saints or guardian angels were no longer allowed, people felt defenseless.[66] As Shakespeare's character, Prospero, says in *The Tempest*:

> Now my charms are all o'erthrown,
> And what strength I have's mine own,
> which is most faint...[67]

It was most often the sermons of both Catholic and Protestant preachers that would instigate a witch hunt. The terrible Basque witch hunt of 1610 began after Fray Domingo de Sardo came to preach about witchcraft. "[T]here were neither witches nor bewitched until they were talked and written about," remarked a contemporary named Salazar.[68] The witch hunts in Salem, Massachusetts, were similarly preceded by the fearful sermons and preaching of Samuel Parris in 1692.[69]

The climate of fear created by churchmen of the Reformation led to countless deaths of accused witches quite independently of inquisitional courts or procedure. For example, in England where there were no inquisitional courts and where witch-hunting offered little or no financial reward, many women were killed for witchcraft by mobs. Instead of following any judicial procedure, these mobs used methods to ascertain guilt of witchcraft such as "swimming a witch," where a woman would be bound and thrown into water to see if she floated. The water, as the medium of baptism, would either reject her and prove her guilty of witchcraft, or the woman would sink and be proven innocent, albeit also dead from drowning.[70]

As people adopted the new belief that the world was the terrifying realm of the devil, they blamed witches for every misfortune. Since the devil created all the ills of the world, his agents—witches—could be blamed for them. Witches were thought by some to have as much if not more power than Christ: they could raise the dead, turn water into wine or milk, control the weather and know the past and future.[71] Witches were held accountable for everything from a failed business venture to a poor emotional state. A Scottish woman, for instance, was accused of witchcraft and burned to death because she was seen stroking a cat at the same time as a nearby batch of beer turned sour.[72] Witches now took the role of scapegoats that had been held by Jews. Any personal misfortune, bad harvest, famine, or plague was seen as their fault.

The social turmoil created by the Reformation intensified witch-hunting. The Reformation diminished the important role of community and placed a greater demand for personal moral perfection. As the communal tradition of mutual help broke

down and the manorial system which had provided more
generously for widows disappeared, many people were left in
need of charity.[73] The guilt one felt after refusing to help a needy
person could be easily transferred onto that needy person by
accusing her of witchcraft. A contemporary writer named
Thomas Ady described a likely situation resulting from a failure
to perform some hitherto customary social obligation:

> *Presently [a householder] cryeth out of some
> poor innocent neighbour that he or she hath
> bewitched him. For, saith he, such an old man
> or woman came lately to my door and desired
> some relief, and I denied it, and God forgive
> me, my heart did rise against her... and pres-
> ently my child, my wife, myself, my horse, my
> cow, my sheep, my sow, my hog, my dog, my
> cat, or somewhat, was thus and thus handled in
> such a strange manner, as I dare swear she is a
> witch, or else how should these things be?*[74]

The most common victims of witchcraft accusations were
those women who resembled the image of the Crone. As the
embodiment of mature feminine power, the old wise woman
threatens a structure which acknowledges only force and domination as avenues of power. The Church never tolerated the image
of the Crone, even in the first centuries when it assimilated the
prevalent images of maiden and mother in the figure of Mary.
Although any woman who attracted attention was likely to be
suspected of witchcraft, either on account of her beauty or

8.3 Witches, as illustrated in this painting of a witch trial, were thought
to possess mighty supernatural powers. The Reformation spread the belief
that the only supernatural power or magic came from the devil and that
God no longer offered any protective magic; the only recourse left to those
in a frightening situation was to do away with the devil's agent, the witch.

because of a noticeable oddness or deformity, the most common victim was the old woman. Poor, older women tended to be the first accused even where witch hunts were driven by inquisitional procedure that profited by targeting wealthier individuals.

Figure 8.4 Old and poor women were most often the first accused of witchcraft.

Old, wise healing women were particular targets for witch-
hunters. "At this day," wrote Reginald Scot in 1584, "it is
indifferent to say in the English tongue, 'she is a witch' or 'she
is a wise woman.'"[75] Common people of pre-reformational
Europe relied upon wise women and men for the treatment of
illness rather than upon churchmen, monks or physicians. Robert
Burton wrote in 1621:

> Sorcerers are too common; cunning men,
> wizards and white witches, as they call them, in
> every village, which, if they be sought unto, will
> help almost all infirmities of body and mind.[76]

By combining their knowledge of medicinal herbs with an
entreaty for divine assistance, these healers provided both more
affordable and most often more effective medicine than was
available elsewhere. Churchmen of the Reformation objected to
the magical nature of this sort of healing, to the preference
people had for it over the healing that the Church or Church-
licensed physicians offered, and to the power that it gave
women.

Until the terror of the witch hunts, most people did not
understand why successful healers should be considered evil.
"Men rather uphold them," wrote John Stearne, "and say why
should any man be questioned for doing good."[77] As a
Bridgettine monk of the early sixteenth century recounted of "the
simple people", "I have heard them say full often myself... 'Sir,
we mean well and do believe well and we think it a good and
charitable deed to heal a sick person or a sick beast'..."[78] And
in 1555 Joan Tyrry asserted that "her doings in healing of man
and beast, by the power of God taught to her by the... fairies, be
both godly and good..."[79]

Indeed, the very invocations used by wise women sound quite
Christian. For example, a 1610 poem recited when picking the
herb vervain, also known as St. Johnswort, reads,

*Hallowed be thou Vervain, as thou growest on
the ground / For in the mount of Calvary there
thou was first found / Thou healest our Saviour,
Jesus Christ, and staunchest his bleeding wound
/ In the name of the Father, the Son, and the
Holy Ghost / I take thee from the ground.*[80]

But in the eyes of orthodox Christians, such healing empowered people to determine the course of their lives instead of submitting helplessly to the will of God. According to churchmen, health should come from God, not from the efforts of human beings. Bishop Hall said, "we that have no power to bid must pray..."[81] Ecclesiastical courts made the customers of witches publicly confess to being "heartily sorry for seeking man's help, and refusing the help of God..."[82] An Elizabethan preacher explained that any healing "is not done by conjuration or divination, as Popish priests profess and practice, but by entreating the Lord humbly in fasting and prayer..."[83] And according to Calvin, no medicine could change the course of events which had already been determined by the Almighty.[84]

Preachers and Church-licensed male physicians tried to fill the function of healer. Yet, their ministrations were often considered ineffective compared to those of a wise woman. The keeper of the Canterbury gaol admitted to freeing an imprisoned wise woman in 1570 because "the witch did more good by her physic than Mr. Pudall and Mr. Wood, being preachers of God's word..."[85] A character in the 1593 *Dialogue concerning Witches* said of a local wise woman that, "she doeth more good in one year than all these scripture men will do so long as they live..."[86]

8.5 Plantain, the herb depicted in this medieval woodcut, was used as a remedy for snake bites and scorpion stings. It was one of many herbs used by healers. By targeting anyone with an understanding of the medicinal properties of plants, the witch-hunts all but destroyed the Western herbal tradition.

Even the Church-licensed male physicians, who relied upon purgings, bleedings, fumigations, leeches, lancets and toxic chemicals such as mercury were little match for an experienced wise woman's knowledge of herbs.[87] As the well-known physician, Paracelsus, asked, "....does not the old nurse very often beat the doctor?"[88] Even Francis Bacon, who demonstrated very little respect for women, thought that "empirics and old women" were "more happy many times in their cures than learned physicians..."[89]

Physicians often attributed their own incompetence to witchcraft. As Thomas Ady wrote:

The reason is ignorantiae pallium maleficium et incantatio—*a cloak for a physician's ignorance. When he cannot find the nature of the disease, he saith the party is bewitched.*[90]

When an illness could not be understood, even the highest body of England, the Royal College of Physicians of London, was known to accept the explanation of witchcraft.[91]

Not surprisingly, churchmen portrayed the healing woman as the most evil of all witches. William Perkins declared, "The most horrible and detestable monster... is the *good* witch."[92] The Church included in its definition of witchcraft anyone with knowledge of herbs for "those who used herbs for cures did so only through a pact with the Devil, either explicit or implicit."[93] Medicine had long been associated with herbs and magic. The Greek and Latin words for medicine, "pharmakeia" and "veneficium," meant both "magic" and "drugs."[94] Mere possession of herbal oils or ointments became grounds for accusation of witchcraft.[95]

A person's healing ability easily led to conviction of witchcraft. In 1590 a woman in North Berwick was suspected of witchcraft because she was curing "all such as were troubled or grieved with any kind of sickness or infirmity."[96] The ailing archbishop of St. Andrews called upon Alison Peirsoun of Byrehill and then, after she had successfully cured him, not only refused to pay her but had her arrested for witchcraft and burned to death.[97] Simply treating unhealthy children by washing them was cause for convicting a Scottish woman of witchcraft.[98]

Witch-hunters also targeted midwives. Orthodox Christians believed the act of giving birth defiled both mother and child. In order to be readmitted to the Church, the mother should be purified through the custom of "churching," which consisted of a quarantine period of forty days if her baby was a boy and eighty days if her baby was a girl, during which both she and her baby were considered heathen. Some thought that a woman who died during this period should be refused a Christian burial. Until the Reformation, midwives were deemed necessary to take care of what was regarded as the nasty business of giving birth, a dishonorable profession best left in the hands of women. But with the Reformation came an increased awareness of the power of midwives. Midwives were now suspected of possessing the skill to abort a fetus, to educate women about techniques of birth control,** and to mitigate a woman's labor pains.[99]

A midwife's likely knowledge of herbs to relieve labor pains was seen as a direct affront to the divinely ordained pain of childbirth. In the eyes of churchmen, God's sentence upon Eve should apply to all women. As stated in Genesis:

> *Unto the woman [God] said, I will greatly multiply thy sorrow and thy conception; in sorrow thou shalt bring forth children; and thy desire shall be to thy husband, and he shall rule over thee.*[100]

** Written evidence of herbal contraceptives dates back at least to 1900 B.C.E. (Noonan, 23). Information about contraceptives during the Middle Ages was passed on by healers and midwives.

To relieve labor pains, as Scottish clergymen put it, would be "vitiating the primal curse of woman..."[101] The introduction of chloroform to help a woman through the pain of labor brought forth the same opposition. According to a New England minister:

> Chloroform is a decoy of Satan, apparently offering itself to bless women; but in the end it will harden society and rob God of the deep earnest cries which arise in time of trouble, for help.[102]

Martin Luther wrote, "If [women] become tired or even die, that does not matter. Let them die in childbirth—that is why they are there."[103] It is hardly surprising that women who not only possessed medicinal knowledge but who used that knowledge to comfort and care for other women would become prime suspects of witchcraft.

How many lives were lost during the centuries of witch-hunting will never be known. Some members of the clergy proudly reported the number of witches they condemned, such as the bishop of Würtzburg who claimed 1900 lives in five years, or the Lutheran prelate Benedict Carpzov who claimed to have sentenced 20,000 devil worshippers.[104] But the vast majority of records have been lost and it is doubtful that such documents would have recorded those killed outside of the courts.

Contemporary accounts hint at the extent of the holocaust. Barbara Walker writes that "the chronicler of Treves reported that in the year 1586, the entire female population of two villages was wiped out by the inquisitors, except for only two women left alive."[105] Around 1600 a man wrote:

> Germany is almost entirely occupied with building fires for the witches... Switzerland has been compelled to wipe out many of her villages on their account. Travelers in Lorraine may see

thousands and thousands of the stakes to which witches are bound.[106]
While the formal persecution of witches raged from about 1450 to 1750, sporadic killing of women on the account of suspected witchcraft has continued into recent times. In 1928 a family of Hungarian peasants was acquitted of beating an old woman to death whom they claimed was a witch. The court based its decision on the ground that the family had acted out of "irresistible compulsion."[107] In 1976 a poor spinster, Elizabeth Hahn, was suspected of witchcraft and of keeping familiars, or devil's agents, in the form of dogs. The neighbors in her small German village ostracized her, threw rocks at her, and threatened to beat her to death before burning her house, badly burning her and killing her animals.[108] A year later in France, an old man was killed for ostensible sorcery.[109] And in 1981, a mob in Mexico stoned a woman to death for her apparent witchcraft which they believed had incited the attack upon Pope John Paul II.[110]

Witch hunts were neither small in scope nor implemented by a few aberrant individuals; the persecution of witches was the official policy of both the Catholic and Protestant Churches.[111] The Church invented the crime of witchcraft, established the process by which to prosecute it, and then insisted that witches be prosecuted. After much of society had rejected witchcraft as a delusion, some of the last to insist upon the validity of witchcraft were among the clergy.[112] Under the pretext of first heresy and then witchcraft, anyone could be disposed of who questioned authority or the Christian view of the world.

Witch-hunting secured the conversion of Europe to orthodox Christianity. Through the terror of the witch hunts, reformational Christians convinced common people to believe that a singular male God reigned from above, that he was separate from the earth, that magic was evil, that there was a powerful devil, and that women were most likely to be his agents. As a by-product of the witch hunts, the field of medicine transferred to exclusively male hands and the Western herbal tradition was largely destroyed. The vast numbers of people brutalized and killed, as well as the impact upon the common perception of God, make the witch hunts one of the darkest chapters of human history.

෧   ෧   ෧

Chapter Nine

Alienation from Nature

Christianity has distanced humanity from nature. As people came to perceive God as a singular supremacy detached from the physical world, they lost their reverence for nature. In Christian eyes, the physical world became the realm of the devil. A society that had once celebrated nature through seasonal festivals began to commemorate biblical events bearing no connection to the earth. Holidays lost much of their celebratory spirit and took on a tone of penance and sorrow. Time, once thought to be cyclical like the seasons, was now perceived to be linear. In their rejection of the cyclical nature of life, orthodox Christians came to focus more upon death than upon life.

Earthliness is synonymous with sinfulness throughout much of the Bible. For example, Colossians states:

> *Put to death therefore what is* earthly *in you: immorality, passion, evil desire, and covetousness, which is idolatry. On account of these the wrath of God is coming.*[1]

A similar message is also found in James: "This [bitter jealousy and selfish ambition in your hearts] is not such as comes down from above, but is earthly, unspiritual and devilish."[2] Paul describes enemies of the cross of Christ as people "whose God is their belly... who mind earthly things."[3] The message is clear: the earth is ungodly.

The Bible suggests that it was God Himself who ordained the antagonism between humanity and nature. God punishes Adam for having eaten from the forbidden tree of knowledge. He says to Adam:

> ...*cursed is the ground for thy sake; in sorrow*
> *shalt thou eat of it all the days of thy life;*
> *Thorns and thistles shall it bring forth to thee;*
> *and thou shalt eat the herb of the field...*[4]

In sharp contrast to earlier traditions in which harmony with nature was a sign of godliness, orthodox Christians understood God to have ordered that the earth become alien and hostile.

Nature was instead seen as the realm of the devil. The Church chose the image of Pan, the Greek god of nature, to portray the devil. The horned, hoofed, and goat-legged man had been associated with a number of fertility figures and had previously been deemed essential to rural well-being. With Pan's guidance, all the mythical creatures of earth were thought to work in harmony: fairies, elves and devas. Pan's skill on the pan-pipes was believed to fill the woods and pastures with enchanted music. His name, "Pan," meant "all" and "bread." But, particularly after the turn of the millennium when the Church authorized specific portrayals of the devil, the vilified Pan came to evoke terror or "panic" as the image of satan.

The perceived separation of nature from God affected the treatment of animals. The canonized thirteenth century scholar, Thomas Aquinas, declared that animals have no afterlife, have no inherent rights, and that "by a most just ordinance of the Creator, both their life and their death are subject to our use."[5] Animals were often thought to be agents of the devil. In his 1991 book, *Replenish the Earth*, Lewis Regenstein writes that:

> ...*in the ten centuries preceding the present one,*
> *there are accounts of the trials, torture and*
> *execution (often by hanging) of hundreds of*
> *animals, mainly by ecclesiastical courts acting*

9.1 The Greek god Pan was associated with nature and fertility before Christians vilified his image as that of the devil.

XXII   *Ciufoli Pastorali.*

> *under the assumption that animals can be used*
> *by the devil to do his work.*[6]

The Inquisition spread the frightening belief in werewolves.[7] And in 1484 Pope Innocent VIII officially ordered pet cats to be burned together with witches, a practice which continued throughout the centuries of witch-hunting.[8]

The belief that animals were agents of the devil contributed to the breakdown in the natural control of rodents. Zealous Christians most frequently targeted cats, wolves, snakes, foxes, chickens and white cocks as animals to be eliminated. Since many of these animals helped control the population of crop-eating and plague-carrying rodents, their elimination intensified outbreaks of plague.[9] To make matters worse, Church-licensed physicians ordered cats and dogs to be killed during times of plague thinking that this would halt infection.[10] Quite the reverse, of course, was true.

The Church spent centuries prohibiting displays of reverence that involved nature. Worship should take place indoors away from the natural elements. Christians destroyed outdoor temples and built churches with roofs in their stead. The Church condemned the veneration of trees and springs, where people would place candles or decorations. The sixth century bishop Martin of Braga asked, "But what is the lighting of wax lights at rocks or trees or wells or crossroads if it is not worship of the devil?"[11]   The General Capitularies of Charlemagne in 789 decreed:

> *With regard to trees, and rocks and springs,*
> *wherever ignorant people put lights or make*
> *other observances, we give notice to everyone*
> *that this is a most evil practice, execrable to*
> *God, and wherever they are found, they are to*
> *be taken away and destroyed.*[12]

Stories attempted to illustrate that the elemental power of trees, groves and nature had submitted to Christ. The fifth century St. Martin of Tours is said to have stood under a revered pine tree as he ordered the tree to be cut down. As the tree was falling on him, he made the sign of the cross and the tree raised itself up again and fell away from him. A similar story involves the eighth century missionary St. Boniface in Hesse. As he chopped at a sacred oak tree, the trunk of the tree is said to have burst into four equal parts and landed in the shape of a cross. And a twelfth century manuscript portrays a scene in which a blind woman is taking an axe to a tree. Despite the presence of the tree's spirits which rise up aghast, a bishop stands beside her blessing her action. Instead of suffering any dire consequences, the woman has her sight restored.[13] According to such stories, the supernatural power of the earth had submitted to that of the celestial Christian God.

But until the Reformation and the witch hunts, most people did not believe this. Unable to convince people of the absence of God in nature, the early Church instead incorporated aspects of the very nature worship it condemned, much in the same way that it developed ecclesiastical magic when it could not eliminate pagan magic. Images of archetypal fertility figures, usually male, sometimes horned, sometimes covered in foliage and disgorging vegetation, found their way into Christian iconography and manuscript illumination. Leaves became a frequent motif in Christian art. Trees which had traditionally been venerated often appeared in churchyards.[14] And church columns were sculpted to simulate tree trunks and perhaps even the mythical tree of life.[15] In its attempt to assimilate people who still revered the divinity manifest in nature, the Church incorporated the very imagery that the orthodox insisted was tied to the devil.

HOLIDAYS

The Church also incorporated annual pagan festivals and holidays, claiming them as Christian. People used to mark the

seasons with celebrations and rituals that integrated their activity with the earth's cycles. The Church placed Christian holidays to coincide with these older festivals in hopes of winning easier acceptance and recognition for its new religion. While the traditional meaning of most of these holidays had nothing to do with orthodox Christianity, the Church usually tolerated the older rituals as it tried to teach a new biblical meaning. It was only during the Reformation that orthodox Christians insisted that the older nature-oriented significance of holidays be abolished.

The cycle of the year, at both the change of the four seasons as well as the height of each season, used to hold great importance. The winter solstice, the darkest day of the year, was a time of new birth. Often it was symbolized by the birth of an annual male fertility figure, a representation of the year's new sun. The height of the winter, midway between the winter solstice and spring equinox, was a time to nurture that new life. Spring was about encouraging fertility, when the sun and earth would unite to later bring forth the abundance of the harvest and the bounty of the hunt. From the summer solstice through autumn the sun's energy transferred to the crops. The height of summer and the fall equinox were celebrations of the year's harvest and bounty. The end of the year when fields lay dormant and the earth seemed to die at the height of autumn was a time to honor the dead and release the past.

By adopting these festivals as Christian, the early Church sought both to win the allegiance of the populace as well as to harness the vitality of such festivals. While there is nothing to indicate the actual time of Jesus's birth, such an event most easily correlated to winter solstice festivals. The Roman celebra-

---

9.2 This medieval woodcut suggests the type of story spread by the Church in hopes of persuading people to abandon their veneration of nature. In such stories, Christians would cut down sacred trees with impunity in order to illustrate how the power of nature had submitted to that of the Christian God.

tion of the birth of the sun god, Mithra, for instance, had also been observed on December 25th. In pre-Christian Egypt and Syria, a winter solstice ritual involved participants who would withdraw into the inner womb-like sanctuary of shrines until midnight at which time they would come forth trumpeting, "The Virgin has brought forth! The light is waxing!"[16] Admonitions against celebrating such a holiday by Tertullian, St. Augustine and Pope Leo I notwithstanding,[17] the Church adopted the winter solstice as Christmas. The birth of God's sun at the solstice easily correlated to the birth of God's son.

An Egyptian winter solstice celebration of the birth of Osiris, the divine representation of masculine fertility, on January sixth became the Christian Epiphany.[18] The Church declared that it signified the manifestation of Jesus's divinity. Yet, the spirit of both Christmas and the Christian Epiphany embodied the timeless celebrations of the winter solstice. The difference between them was due more to a difference in calendars than a difference in meaning; the Egyptian calendar was twelve days behind the Julian calendar.[19] The dates of many current holidays do not fall exactly on the solstice, equinox, or height of the season for a similar reason. Means of tracking time varied tremendously. Our present calendar was not completely adopted in England until 1751, in Russia until 1919, or in China until 1949.[20]

Festivals to mark the height of winter also found their way into Christianity. Whether celebrated on the second or fourteenth of February, celebrations in honor of feminine faces of divinity such as Brigit and Venus, who encouraged art, poetry, healing, fire and wisdom, became the Christian Candlemas.[21] Over time, however, the holiday lost the meaning of nourishing creativity and inspiration, and instead commemorated the end of Mary's

---

The following chart outlines the seasonal celebrations and the correlating Christian holiday.

TIME OF YEAR	PRE-CHRISTIAN OR PAGAN TRADITION	CHRISTIAN ADAPTATION
Winter Solstice	The feminine gives birth to the sun or a masculine fertility figure. Often celebrated with yule fires, processions of light, tree decorating.	Christmas Epiphany
Winter Season	A time of nurturing and honoring inspiration and creativity. Common practices involving festivals of light, wearing animal masks and skins in hopes of augmenting the coming year's supply.	Candlemas
Spring Equinox	The sun is resurrected and gains prominence over the night. Fertility celebrations involving symbols such as the egg and the prolific hare.	Easter
Spring Season	The mating of the earth and sky from which will come the year's harvest. Often celebrated with maypole dancing, decorating with new foliage.	Pentecost Feast of the Ascension
Summer Solstice	The peak of the sun's light. Celebrated with large bonfires, burning fragrant herbs, decorating with flowers.	Feast of Saint John
Summer Season	The sun's energy transfers to the crops. Ritual blessings of the harvest, herbs, fields, mountains, and ocean. Making figures of dolls or grain.	Assumption Day
Fall Equinox	A time of gratitude for the harvest. Feasts and decorating with fall fruits, grains and vegetables.	Michaelmas Nativity of Mary
Fall Season	Acknowledgment of the year's completion. Honoring the dead, honoring and releasing the past.	All Soul's Day All Saint's Day

forty day period of purification after having given birth.

The Church adopted spring equinox celebrations as Easter. As this time had already been one of celebrating the sun's resurrection and return to prominence, celebrating the resurrection of the son of God required no great change in understanding. In fact, the Easter celebrations were so similar to earlier celebrations —particularly those which recognized the resurrection of the Babylonian Adonis, the Greek Apollo and the Roman Attis—that a bitter controversy arose with pagans claiming that the Christian Easter celebration was a spurious imitation of the ancient traditions.[22] Vernal equinox bonfires, originally prohibited by the Church, found their way as Easter fires into the official liturgy of Rome by the ninth century.[23] Fertility symbols associated with spring, such as the egg and the incredibly prolific rabbit, survived as well.

Yet, as Christianity spread, festivals of spring and summer gradually lost their original meaning. The height of spring became Pentecost or Whitsunday, an observance not of fertility, but of the biblical event when people spoke in tongues, and a commemoration of the birth of the Church. The summer solstice no longer was to recognize the culmination of the sun's light, but rather was to honor St. John who had baptized Christ. Celebrations of the summer season became holidays for the Virgin Mary such as "Our Lady's Herb Day" and Assumption Day, the day when Mary was "assumed" into heaven.[24]

Fall equinox celebrations were incorporated as Michaelmas (the feast of the archangel Michael, the conqueror of satan) and the Nativity of Mary. Gratitude for the harvest, and the blessing of the year's medicinal herbs, of nearby mountains, or of the ocean remained a part of these autumn holidays. To this day, shrines of Mary covered in ears of corn resembling the older

---

9.3 Much of the pre-Christian reverence for feminine divinity transferred to the worship of the Virgin Mary and resulted in holidays in her honor throughout the year.

pagan figures of grain can be found in autumn.[25]

The height of fall, the end of the earth's annual cycle, was believed to be a time when the veil that separates the world of the living from the world of the dead becomes very thin. Despite Church attempts to prevent the celebration of this holiday, by the ninth century the feast of All Saints Day had been moved to November first and by 1045 the monasteries of Cluny had begun to observe the time as a "day of all the departed ones."[26] The earlier nature-oriented significance of the season survived more fully, however, in the secular celebration of Halloween.

Pagans also observed the cycles of the moon. Often these festivals involved veneration for feminine facets of God. Christian theologians condemned celebrations observing the cycles of the moon, called la Luna, as madness or "lunacy," while St. Augustine denounced women's dances in honor of the new moon as "impudent and filthy."[27] When the Church could not halt such celebrations, however, it again incorporated them into the Christian calendar, usually under the guise of honoring Mary. The Church formally recognized the following: the day when St. Anne conceived Mary, December 8th; the day Mary was born, September 8th; the day Jesus's conception was announced to Mary, also called the Annunciation, March 25th; the day Mary was purified from having given birth, February 2nd or 14th; and the day Mary was assumed into heaven, or the Assumption, August 15th. Unofficial celebrations of Mary were even more numerous.

CELEBRATION

While adopting nature-oriented festivals helped garner membership for the early Church, the celebratory spirit of these festivals conflicted with the asceticism and solemnity of the orthodox. As the sixteenth century Guillaume Briçonnet warned,

"[H]olidays are not for the pleasure of the body, but for the salvation of the soul; not for laughter and frolic, but for weeping."[28] With the Reformation, both Protestant and Catholic Churches attempted to abolish not only the nature oriented practices of festivals but also the joyful spirit that accompanied them. Holidays were now to be strict commemorations of biblical events that had no connection to the earth's seasons.

The Church identified pagan practices as those which displayed either enjoyment or a connection with nature. Reverence for nature was so closely linked with expressions of joy that St. Augustine thought that the word "jubilation" derived from *jubilus*, the song hummed by those tending vines and olives.[29] The ninth century Synod of Rome reported that "Many people, mostly women, come to church on Sundays and holy days not to attend the Mass but to dance, sing broad songs, and do other such pagan things."[30] The *Catéchisme de Meaux* describes pagan practices:

> *Dancing round the fire, playing, holding feasts,*
> *singing vulgar songs, throwing grasses over the*
> *fire, gathering grasses before midnight or before*
> *breakfast, wearing grasses, keeping them for the*
> *whole year, keeping brands or cinders from the*
> *fire and the like...*[31]

Dancing was particularly offensive to orthodox Christians. In the sixth and seventh centuries ecclesiastical dancing was prohibited as being too sensual and too much enjoyed by women. Inquisitors claimed that both women and devil-worshippers danced.[32] Dancing was a sign of spiritual decay to New England's Puritan ministers who in 1684 published a pamphlet entitled *An Arrow against Profane and Promiscuous Dancing, drawn out of the Quiver of the Scriptures.*[33] An eighteenth century missionary hymn warns that satan

> *...slithers through the flesh*
> *Of dancing men and dames*

To hold them in the mesh
Of his hot and am'rous flames.[34]

Certainly not all Christians agreed with the orthodox. In the *Acts of John*, for instance, Jesus danced and said:

To the Universe belongs the dancer, He who
does not dance does not know what happens.
Now if you follow my dance, see yourself in
me.[35]

To the orthodox, neither nature nor physical pleasure were imbued with God's presence; both were of the devil. The Church had long condemned sensual pleasure as ungodly. As the twelfth century Bishop of Chartres, Sir John of Salisbury, declared:

Who except one b•reft of sense would approve
sensual pleasure itself, which is illicit, wallows
in filthiness, is something that men censure, and
that God without doubt condemns?[36]

Holidays had involved such gaiety and pleasure that the Bishop of Autun wrote in 1657, "It is not appropriate to multiply holidays of obligation for fear of multiplying the occasions of sin..."[37]

With the Reformation came the demand to curtail or abolish the celebratory and nature-oriented character of holidays. Laughter and revelry were seen as inappropriate for Christians engaged in daily combat with satan. Orthodox Christians wanted to ban maypoles and Sunday dancing, bagpipes and fiddlers accompanying bridal couples to Church, the throwing of corn, and the distribution of doles to the poor as "superstitious and heathenical."[38] Wedding celebrations, according to New England magistrates and ministers, should not result in "riotous or immodest irregularities."[39] A law in 1639 prohibited the custom of drinking toasts or health-drinking as an "abominable" pagan practice.[40] One should not adjourn to the tavern after meetings, and nature-oriented occasions such as harvest huskings should not degenerate into merrymaking occasions.[41]

In 1647 the English Parliament ordered that Christmas, along with other pagan holidays, should cease to be observed. A 1652 Parliamentary act repeated that "no observance shall be had on the five-and-twentieth of December, commonly called Christmas day; nor any solemnity used or exercised in churches in respect thereof."[42]   Market was to be kept and stores were to remain open on Christmas day.[43] In New England, where celebrating Christmas was considered a criminal offense and remained forbidden until the second half of the nineteenth century, a person caught celebrating Christmas was liable to end up at the stocks or the whipping post.[44] Factory owners changed starting hours to 5:00 a.m. on Christmas day and threatened termination for those who were tardy. As late as 1870 in Boston, students who failed to attend public schools on Christmas were punished by public dismissal.[45]

Practices involving nature at holidays were curtailed. Orthodox Christians ceased Church processions around towns and fields, which were intended to bless crops, to ask for a change in weather, or to appeal for protection against insects. They suppressed the practice of collecting branches, foliage and flowers to be taken back to the church.[46] The 1683 Addendum to the constitution of the diocese of Annecy read:

> ...we order the people, under pain of excommu-
> nication, to suppress and abolish entirely the
> torches and fires customarily lit on the first
> Sunday of Lent... and the masquerades... which
> are merely shameful relics of Paganism.[47]

Efforts to abolish paganism centered upon doing away with reverence and enjoyment of both nature and feminine energy. Not surprisingly, the imagery used in reference to nature often had strong sexual overtones. Francis Bacon, whose aim was "to endeavor to establish the power and dominion of the human race itself over the universe," frequently used such imagery.[48] In his book *The Rebirth of Nature*, Rupert Sheldrake writes,

Using metaphors derived from contemporary techniques of interrogation and torture of witches, [Francis Bacon] proclaimed that nature 'exhibits herself more clearly under the trials and vexations of art [mechanical devices] than when left to herself.' In the inquisition of truth, nature's secret 'holes and corners' were to be entered and penetrated. Nature was to be 'bound into service' and made a 'slave' and 'put in constraint.' She would be 'dissected,' and by the mechanical arts and the hand of man, she could be 'forced out of her natural state and squeezed and moulded,' so that 'human knowledge and human power meet as one.[49]

Nature was to be conquered, not enjoyed and certainly not revered.

A grim cheerlessness came to distinguish Christians. Already in the twelfth century the Abbot, Ruppert of Deutz, tried to defend the somberness of a Christian holiday:

It is not a fast to make us sad or darken our hearts, but it rather brightens the solemnity of the Holy Spirit's arrival; for the sweetness of the Spirit of God makes the faithful loathe the pleasures of earthly food.[50]

By the eighteenth century, "boring" and "pious" were thought to be synonymous.[51] In 1746 Diderot described the extremes of Christian "unhappiness":

What cries! what shrieks! what groans! Who has imprisoned all these woeful corpses? What crimes have all these wretches committed? Some are beating their breasts with stones, others are

---

9.4 Orthodox Christians, particularly during the Reformation, curtailed large festivals and celebrations. In some countries even Christmas, along with other "pagan" holidays, was banned.

> *tearing bodies with hooks of are beating their*
> *breasts with iron; remorse, pain and death lurk*
> *in their eyes...* "[52]

As one man commented during the Reformation, "It was never merry England since we were impressed to come to the church."[53]

TIME

Christians encouraged a new concept of time that similarly had no connection to nature's cycles. Up until the Reformation, most people understood time to be cyclical. Reformational Christians, however, adopted St. Augustine's idea of linear time. Augustine described the pagan theory of cycles, *circuitus temporum*, as:

> *...those argumentations whereby the infidel seeks*
> *to undermine our simple faith, dragging us from*
> *the straight road and compelling us to walk with*
> *him on the wheel.*[54]

Like the theory of reincarnation, the idea of cyclical time denied the uniqueness and finality of Jesus Christ.[55] If time spirals around, providing repeated opportunities to grow and change, then the spirit of Jesus's life and resurrection could theoretically be experienced by anyone at anytime, regardless of

---

9.5 As people during the Reformation came to perceive the nature of time to be linear rather than cyclical, time seemed to become an unrelenting task-master, demanding that one spend every moment fulfilling one's duties and obligations. This sixteenth century allegorical representation shows time rewarding industry and punishing indolence. The concept of linear time also frightened many into thinking that there is but one chance to turn to God, rather than the numerous opportunities inherent in the concept of cyclical time.

apostolic succession or hierarchical rank. Moreover, if time is cyclical, life might not consist of just one frightening chance to repent or else to be forever damned, but rather of unlimited opportunities to develop a closer relationship with God. Controlling people is more difficult when they believe that there are many means and opportunities to return to God other than simply the one that the Church offers.

Reformational Christians disparaged the beliefs and practices associated with the concept of cyclical time. They opposed the belief in lucky and unlucky days, such as that it was unlucky to marry during a waning moon or that a sin committed on a holy day was worse than one committed at another time. Time should move evenly in a straight line without the disruptions and irregularity of changing seasons; six working days should always be followed by a sabbath resting day throughout the year.[56] As one Puritan character in a contemporary satire declares:

> ...it was passing folly
> To think one day more than another holy...[57]

The pendulum clock was invented in 1657 as a testimony to the belief that minutes were uniform in duration. By 1714, the new concept of even, linear time had become familiar enough for a man to write in reference to the belief in lucky and unlucky days that "some weak and ignorant persons may perhaps regard such things, but men of understanding despise them..."[58] As with so many elements of orthodox Christianity, the concept of linear time was adopted by common people only after the Reformation.

DEATH

Orthodox Christians repudiated the cyclical nature of physical life as well. Passages in the New Testament exhibit disdain for the cycle of life: "Then when lust hath conceived, it bringeth forth sin: and sin, when it is finished, bringeth forth death."[59]

By fostering an alienation from sex, birth, and the physical body, orthodox Christians came to focus most intently upon death, not only as a tool to evoke fear but also as an end in itself.

Christian theologians understood sex, at best, to be permissible if engaged in solely for purposes of procreation—at worst, to be a mortal sin. Yet, they also believed that the birthing of a child was an ungodly act. The Church, with its licensed physicians, spurned the field of midwifery. A woman who died in labor or in child-bed was sometimes refused a Christian burial.[60] Purifying or "churching" a woman for 40 to 80 days after she gave birth was deemed essential if a she was to be readmitted into the Church and proper Christian society. Even the Virgin Mary—in some people's eyes—needed to be purified after having brought Jesus into the world.

Orthodox Christianity encouraged an alienation from the physical body itself. God's presence, it was believed, was not to be found in the physical world. Paul wrote in Corinthians, "therefore we are always confident, knowing that, whilst we are at home in the body, we are absent from the Lord."[61] The Bible affirms that meaningful, spiritual life is found only when one is detached from the physical body: "For if ye live after the flesh, ye shall die: but if ye through the Spirit do mortify the deeds of the body, ye shall live."[62] "For to be carnally minded is death; but to be spiritually minded is life and peace."[63] Physical life is equated with sin and spiritual decay, while physical death and a repudiation of physical well-being is thought to bring spiritual life.

A disregard for the well-being of the physical body characterized orthodox Christian behavior from the fall of the Roman Empire when aqueduct systems, bathing houses and hygiene were held in contempt and neglected. Protestants and reformed Catholics attempted to outdo one another in their negligence of bodily hygiene. As the Augustinian priest and chaplain to the King of Poland declared:

Follow Our Lord's example, and hate your body;
if you love it, strive to lose it, says Holy Scrip-
ture, in order to save it; if you wish to make
peace with it, always go armed, always wage
war against it; treat it like a slave, or soon you
yourself shall be its unhappy slave.[64]

In the Christian world the very word "carnal," which means simply "of or relating to the body,"[65] took on the meaning of sin and immorality.

Orthodox Christians also often contended that death was not a natural part of life but rather was a punishment. St. Augustine argued that death existed only as a punishment for sin:

Wherefore we must say that the first men were
indeed so created, that if they had not sinned,
they would not have experienced any kind of
death; but that, having become sinners, they
were so punished with death, that whatsoever
sprang from their stock should also be punished
with the same death.[66]

And:

...therefore it is agreed among all Christians
who truthfully hold the catholic faith, that we
are subject to the death of the body, not by the
law of nature, by which God ordained no death
for man, but by His righteous infliction on
account of sin...[67]

Just as Augustine had argued that sin had created sexual desire, so he also believed that sin had created death.

Death, in the eyes of the orthodox, was to be conquered. Paul wrote in I Corinthians, "The last enemy that shall be destroyed is death."[68] St. Ignatius, the bishop of Antioch, describes how the Apostles "despised death, and were found to rise above death."[69] Christian faith is believed to imbue one with power over death. In the Gospel of Luke, Jesus says:

But they which shall be accounted worthy to
obtain that world, and the resurrection from the
dead, neither marry, nor are given in marriage:
Neither can they die any more; *for they are*
equal unto angels; and are the children of God,
being the children of the resurrection.[70]

Instead of accepting death as a natural part of the life cycle, orthodox Christians used death as a tool to evoke fear in people. The fourth century St. Pachomius advised his monks: "Above all, let us always keep our last day before our eyes and let us always fear everlasting torment."[71] St. Benedict's rule instructs: "Dread the Day of Judgment, fear Hell, desire eternal life with entirely spiritual ardour, keep the possibility of death ever before your eyes."[72] The ancient concept of an underworld where one would go after death for rest and rejuvenation became the frightening Christian idea of hell, a place filled with fire and brimstone where one endures eternal pain and agony. Death, particularly in a context where there is but one life and one chance to do the right thing, became a terrifying prospect.

It took the Church a long time, however, to teach such an orthodox understanding of death. The Church initially made Christianity comprehensible to the populace by incorporating pre-Christian ideas. The concept of purgatory adopted by the medieval Church mitigated the harshness of orthodox ideology. Instead of being sent directly to heaven or hell after death, one's soul could go to purgatory, an intermediate place, to do penance and be punished for sins before hopefully being allowed into heaven.[73] Such a concept also proved quite lucrative for the Church. By maintaining that it could influence the destiny of these souls, the Church collected a good deal of medieval society's money for its services on behalf of those in purgatory.

With the spread of orthodox Christianity during the Reformation, however, all activities that dealt with death as a natural part of life were to be isolated and reviled. No longer should one think of departed ones as being in purgatory; people would be judged immediately upon dying and sent directly to heaven or hell. A person's death should no longer be made into an important occasion or seen as part of a natural cycle. Funerals went from being large community events to small family affairs.[74] Orthodox Christians tried to ban the tolling of Church bells at funerals and the use of special mourning garments.[75] Cemeteries, once busy meeting places, should be segregated from everyday life. Dancing, games, and commercial activities in cemeteries were routinely forbidden.[76] A 1701 city ordinance in New England prohibited making coffins, digging graves or holding funerals on the Sabbath as acts that profaned the holy day.[77]

Ironically, in attempting to conquer death and isolate it from life, orthodox Christianity fostered a preoccupation with death. Augustine perceived life to be wholly overshadowed by death. "For no sooner do we begin to live in this dying body, than we begin to move ceaselessly towards death."[78] Death, according to the orthodox, could bring salvation. Augustine wrote:

> But now, by the greater and more admirable grace of the Savior the punishment of sin is turned to the service of righteousness. For then it was proclaimed to man, 'If thou sinnest, thou shalt die'; now it is said to the martyr, 'Die, that thou sin not.' Then it was said, 'If ye transgress the commandments, ye shall die'; now it is said, 'If ye decline death, ye transgress the commandment.'[79]

Orthodox Christians, in their effort to conquer it, often ended up glorifying death. Jesus's most valuable act was understood to be, not his miracles of healing or his message of love and peace, but rather his act of dying. The Bible states that "the day of death [is better] than the day of one's birth."[80]   It became customary to call a Martyr's day of death his or her "birthday."[81] Augustine tried to explain why death had taken on such an elevated character:

> Not that death, which was before an evil, has
> become good, but only that God has granted to
> faith this grace, that death, which is the admit-
> ted opposite to life, should become the instru-
> ment by which life is reached.[82]

St. John Cimacus of the seventh century wrote, "Just as bread is the most necessary of all foods, so meditation on death is the most important of all actions."[83] And the prominent St. John Chrysostom declared that "the principal character [of a Christian] is to desire and love death."[84] Orthodox Christianity had taken on the character of a death cult.

A preoccupation with death overshadowed Christian attitudes towards the world at large. Understanding earthly, physical life to be inimical to spirituality fostered a zealous anticipation of the end of the world. Christians expected God to revisit the earth in a second coming to usher in the end times. In the canonized *Gospel of Matthew*, Jesus gives the impression that such an end may be short at hand: "Truly, I say to you, there are some standing here who will not taste death before they see the Son of Man coming in his kingdom."[85] Periodic waves of expecting the destruction of the world marked Christian history. During the Reformation in England, for example, eighty books were published on the subject of the world's end.[86]

Orthodox Christianity changed the way people think about the earth and the natural environment. When God is believed to reign from above, nature is understood to be distant from, if not devoid of, God's presence. Such a world view led to dramatic changes in the meaning of holidays, the character of those holidays, and the perception of time, all of which were alienated from the earth's seasonal cycles. The facets of human life which speak of a connection to cycles, such as birth, sex, and death were disparaged. Rather than appreciating the natural life cycle, orthodox Christians denied that cycle entirely and became preoccupied with death.

಄ ಄ ಄

Chapter Ten

A World Without God

1600 - the Present

Orthodox Christianity fostered humanity's shift towards a world view that pays little heed to the idea of divinity. By teaching that the earthly realm is devoid of sanctity, Christians built the ideological foundation for modern society. Modern thinkers perpetuated the concepts of orthodox Christianity, providing scientific validation for the belief in hierarchy, domination and struggle. With the approach of the twenty-first century, however, there is a growing awareness not only of the drawbacks of such concepts, but also of their limited scientific accuracy.

Soon after people accepted the belief that God no longer wielded supernatural power in the physical world, it became common, particularly among the educated, to believe that the devil also exercised no such power. Once the idea of divine magic had been rejected, it was easy to accept that no magic, divine or evil, operates in the physical realm. Physical reality was instead perceived to be the mechanistic operation of inanimate components functioning entirely upon rational and definable laws, similar to that of a huge clock. As Shakespeare's character Lafew says of the age:

> *They say miracles are past; and we have our*
> *philosophical persons, to make modern and*

familiar, things supernatural and causeless.¹

This new perception and world view characterized what has been called the "Age of Enlightenment." Lacking the passionate creativity of the Renaissance, the Enlightenment was inspired by seventeenth century thinkers such as Galileo, René Descartes, Johannes Kepler, Isaac Newton, Francis Bacon, Benedict Spinoza, and John Locke. While most still believed that God had originally created the world, they now thought that the universe functioned according to comprehensive laws which required no further intervention on God's part.

These new beliefs and attitudes mirrored those of orthodox Christianity. As orthodox Christians believed there to be a division between heaven and earth, so scientists perceived there to be a similar division, coined by Descartes as that between mind and matter. As Christians believed God to be detached from the physical world, so scientists thought that consciousness and physical reality were detached from one another. Although orthodox Christianity and modern thinkers differed in their belief about the devil, both understood the physical world as a realm devoid of divinity and sanctity.

The belief that the physical world functioned independently of consciousness found new validation in Newton's laws. His laws of motion and of gravity depicted a universe which operated upon a thoroughly impartial, mechanical and deterministic basis. Newton based all of his work upon experimental evidence as a testimony to the belief that matter was devoid of supernatural influence and consciousness; since the thoughts of the person conducting the experiment would have no impact upon matter, every experiment's result should be able to be duplicated.² In other words, he believed that it was possible for a person to observe a physical phenomenon without influencing it. Accepting the orthodox Christian idea that God no longer had impact upon the physical world, modern thinkers concurred that human consciousness similarly did not influence physical phenomena.

10.1 This woodcut illustrates the shift in humanity's perception of the universe. As the image suggests, it was as if people moved from a magical world of personified forces, to an indifferent, mechanical world which functioned much like a clock. The workings of the universe came to be attributed not to magic or supernatural intervention, but to Newton's laws of gravity and motion.

SIR ISAAC NEWTON.

OB, 1727.

Scientists and philosophers also embraced the concept of hierarchy and applied it to their work. Hierarchical order requires all components to be separated and ranked according to their superiority or inferiority; it focuses upon a component's difference rather than upon its supportive relationship and connection to the whole. Scientists similarly focused upon the separation, isolation and analysis of increasingly smaller particles. Little attention was given to the relationship connecting a component to its surrounding elements or environment.

Modern philosophy echoed the same idea with the belief that reality emanated from and was caused by insignificant and random events rather than from and by larger, intentional consciousness. Descartes coined the belief with his famous phrase *Cogito ergo sum*, "I think, therefore I am." The smaller, less significant act of thinking leads to the larger, more significant reality of being. While many still believed that God originally created the universe, most now thought that truth would be found, not by focusing upon or trying to understand God's plan or intention, but by understanding the small, separate, mechanical parts of the universe.

Belief in the necessity of domination and struggle, as well as in the absence of divine intervention, found new justification in Charles Darwin's theory of evolution. As orthodox Christianity, particularly during the Reformation, stressed the nobility of struggle and the sinfulness of magic and supernatural assistance, so Darwin portrayed the natural world as a place where struggle and competition characterize every aspect of "the great and complex battle of life." Struggle, according to Darwin, was essential to maintaining the natural order and preventing the disastrous explosion of any one population.

10.2 Sir Isaac Newton. His scientific laws of gravity and motion lent validation to the orthodox Christian belief that God no longer worked miracles or intervened in the physical world.

While orthodox Christians maintained that domination and struggle were necessary to sustain a divine hierarchy, Darwin believed the same qualities necessary to uphold a natural hierarchy:

> *Man, like every other animal, has no doubt advanced to his present high condition through a struggle for existence consequent on his rapid multiplication; and if he is to advance still higher, it is to be feared that he must remain subject to severe struggle. Otherwise he would sink into indolence, and the more gifted men would not be more successful in the battle of life than the less gifted.*[3]

Both orthodox Christians and modern thinkers deemed hierarchy essential, whether that hierarchy differentiated human beings according to their proximity to God or according to their ability to survive. Darwin's theories provided a new rationalization for subjugating people according to race or gender; they were now believed to be "naturally" weaker.

Despite their similarities, orthodox Christianity is often thought to oppose modern science and thought. The Catholic Church did continue its tradition of hindering scholarly work by persecuting Galileo through the Inquisition and by opposing much of Newton's work.* And, indeed, there were ideological differences between orthodox Christians and modern thinkers.

---

* While Galileo's heliocentric theory challenged the Church's theory that the sun revolved around the earth, Newton's work challenged the basis for Catholic authority. His insistence upon the possibility of experimentally verifying physical phenomenon called into question the basis for the Church's claim to authority. The authority of the Catholic Church rests upon apostolic succession, the idea that truth has been revealed only during the one-time event of Jesus's flesh-and-bone resurrection and, consequently, that truth is accessible only through the successors of the Apostles who witnessed the resurrection.

Modern thinkers, for example, dismissed the idea that the devil exercised supernatural influence, while the orthodox fervently insisted upon it. Darwin's theory of evolution does differ from the Christian concept of creation. Yet, the premise of modern thought, that the universe functioned without divine intervention or magic, was one that both Catholics and Protestants themselves had fiercely advocated.

Even Charles Darwin did not believe that his work opposed the tenets of orthodox Christianity. Reformational Christians would certainly have agreed with him that physical reality functions "not by miraculous acts of creation" but rather through struggle and competition.[4] Darwin wrote in *The Origin of Species*, "I see no good reason why the views given in this volume should shock the religious feelings of any one." He describes how a religious man:

> *...learnt to see that it is just as noble a concep-*
> *tion of the Deity to believe that He created a few*
> *original forms capable of self-development into*
> *other and needful forms, as to believe that He*
> *required a fresh act of creation to supply the*
> *voids caused by the action of His laws.[5]*

Modern thought supported orthodox Christian concepts far more than it contradicted them.

However, while Darwin believed that his work did not oppose the concept of an almighty God, his theories were used by others to deny even a remote creator. Atheism simply extended the Christian idea that God is distant and removed from the physical world. Once people accepted that, it was not difficult to believe that God did not exist at all. The seeds of atheism also grew in popularity as a reaction to the brutality of the witch hunts. People began to argue that religion did not guarantee a moral conscience and that an absence of religious conviction did not

10.3 Sir Charles Darwin. The orthodox Christian belief in the necessity of hierarchy, domination and struggle found new justification in Darwin's work.

lead to moral depravity. The late seventeenth century *Historical and Critical Dictionary*, for instance, affirmed that "atheism does not necessarily lead to the corruption of mores."[6]

Atheism does, however, threaten the underpinnings of a fear-based social order. Although God may have been relegated to a more distant position in heaven, fear of His punishment was still thought to enforce individual morality. Many thought that the judicial system depended upon fear. In his book *Obstruction of Justice By Religion*, Frank Swancara notes that:

> ...*the judges who moulded the common law thought that one who does not believe in nor fear Divine punishment after death cannot be trusted as a witness in a court of law.*[7]

Most thinkers of the Enlightenment found atheism as threatening as did orthodox Christians. Voltaire asked,

> *What restraint, after all, could be imposed on covetousness, on the secret transgressions committed with impunity, other than the idea of an eternal master whose eye is upon us and who will judge even our most private thoughts?*[8]

And John Locke wrote:

> *Those are not at all to be tolerated who deny the being of a God. Promises, covenants, and oaths, which are the bonds of human society, can have no hold upon an atheist.*[9]

Both orthodox Christianity and modern thinkers, while willing to dispense with the belief in magic and miracles, still relied upon the belief in God's fearful punishment.

Modern thought most often validated Christian tenets. The perception that the universe operates like a machine or a clock corroborated St. Augustine's contention that human beings have no free will. In his book *The Dancing Wu Li Masters*, Gary Zukav writes:

If we are to accept the mechanistic determination of Newtonian physics—if the universe really is a great machine—then from the moment that the universe was created and set into motion, everything that was to happen in it already was determined.

According to this philosophy, we may seem to have a will of our own and the ability to alter the course of events in our lives, but we do not. Everything, from the beginning of time, has been predetermined, including our illusion of having a free will. The universe is a prerecorded tape playing itself out in the only way that it can. The status of men is immeasurably more dismal than it was before the advent of science. The Great Machine runs blindly on, and all things in it are but cogs.[10]

Whether on account of determinism or because of humanity's lowly position within a divine hierarchy, people continued to believe that the individual has little inherent power or free will

Science adopted the same ideas that encouraged Christians to treat the natural environment as a realm devoid of sanctity. Fritjof Capra describes how the division between mind and matter

...allowed scientists to treat matter as dead and completely separate from themselves, and to see the material world as a multitude of different objects assembled into a huge machine... From the second half of the seventeenth to the end of the nineteenth century, the mechanistic... model of the universe dominated all scientific thought. It was paralleled by the image of a monarchial God who ruled the world from above by imposing his divine law on it.[11]

By advocating a division between heavenly and earthly realms, or between mind and matter, both Christians and modern thinkers disassociated themselves from the physical world.

Many concepts which originated in orthodox Christian ideology and found validation among modern thinkers are now, at the end of the twentieth century, proving to be of limited scientific accuracy. Scientific discoveries, most notably in quantum mechanics, have shown classical physics to be severely limited in its capacity to explain the workings of the universe. The principles and laws that appear to govern the mechanistic, deterministic universal machine simply do not apply to sub-atomic particles. Sub-atomic particles defy attempts to establish them absolutely within time and space. The physicist Stephen Hawking observes that this phenomenon, called the uncertainty principle

> ...signaled an end to [the] dream of a theory of science, a model of the universe that would be completely deterministic: one certainly cannot predict future events exactly if one cannot even measure the present state of the universe pre-cisely![12]

The belief that the universe functions upon entirely rational and definable laws is now in question. While Newton thought that, given enough information, one can absolutely determine the outcome of an event, quantum mechanics has shown that at best one can know only the *probability* of any outcome.[13] Gary Zukav describes what became known as the Copenhagen Interpretation:

> ...scientists attempting to formulate a consistent physics were forced by their own findings to acknowledge that a complete understanding of reality lies beyond the capabilities of rational thought.[14]

Recent science has also challenged the belief that physical matter is completely inanimate, unresponsive, and substantive.

In their explorations of wave functions, scientists have found physical reality to be both "idea-like" and "matter-like."[15] The division between mind and matter, which corroborated the Christian division between heaven and earth, is not true scientifically. The physical world is not composed of solid, inert, and inanimate matter as was thought in classical physics. The physicist Henry Stapp writes:

> If the attitude of quantum mechanics is correct ...then there is no substantive physical world, in the usual sense of this term. The conclusion here is not the weak conclusion that there may not be a substantive physical world but rather that there definitely is not a substantive physical world.[16]

Another physicist, E.H. Walker writes:

> Consciousness may be associated with all quantum mechanical processes... since everything that occurs is ultimately the result of one or more quantum mechanical events, the universe is 'inhabited' by an almost unlimited number of rather discrete conscious, usually nonthinking entities that are responsible for the detailed working of the universe.[17]

Such findings contradict the belief in the separation of mind and matter.

Both the division between mind and matter and the idea that the earth is devoid of consciousness are also called into question by the more recent Gaia theory. Put forward primarily by James Lovelock, the Gaia theory suggests that the earth may be a self-regulating system. Such a theory explains the relative constancy of the earth's climate, the surprisingly moderate amounts of salt in the oceans and the steady level of oxygen, all of which permit life to thrive.[18] It may not be an accident or the result of random chance that the earth has maintained an environment capable of supporting life. Rather, the earth's activities may be the result of self-regulating behavior, which suggests the existence of consciousness.

Even the classical means of verifying truth are now considered erroneous. Newton believed that since experiments relating to physical matter involved inanimate particles which lacked consciousness, all results from such experiments should be repeatable; the person conducting the experiment could act as an objective observer without having any impact upon the physical matter. The possibility of such an objective observer, however, now no longer seems feasible; quantum mechanics has shown that the simple act of observation does have impact upon the matter observed. The physicist John Wheeler writes:

> May the universe in some strange sense be *'brought into being'* by the participation of those who participate?... *'Participator'* is the incontrovertible new concept given by quantum mechanics. It strikes down the term *'observer'* of classical theory, the man who stands safely behind the thick glass wall and watches what goes on without taking part. It can't be done, quantum mechanics says.[19]

Recent scientific discoveries are proving the Newtonian and Cartesian perception of a mechanistic universe, which developed out of the belief that God no longer inhabited the world, to be of limited accuracy.

The modern scientific method, which emphasizes dissecting and analyzing ever smaller components and echoes the Christian attempt to segregate hierarchical components, is also being reconsidered. Recent science suggests that truth might better be found, not just by focusing upon the separation and segregation of components, but also by understanding the interrelatedness of such components within a larger system. "Parts," as the physicist David Bohm explains,

...are seen to be in immediate connection, in which their dynamical relationships depend, in an irreducible way, on the state of the whole system (and, indeed, on that of broader systems in which they are contained, extending ultimately and in principle to the entire universe). Thus, one is led to a new notion of unbroken whole-ness *which denies the classical idea of analyzability of the world into separately and independently existent parts...*[20]

Understanding the relationship of matter to the whole system might reveal more truth than analyzing the isolated components of that matter. Understanding how components work together might be more productive than ordering those components hierarchically.

The orthodox insistence upon the inherent value of struggle, which found renewed justification in Darwin's ideas, might also warrant revaluation. The Gaia theory, which proposes that the earth may be a self-regulating system, suggests that living organisms form symbiotic living patterns in order to bring about mutually beneficial situations. It suggests that order and evolution come about, not only through domination, struggle and competition as both orthodox Christianity and Darwinian theory imply, but also through cooperation.

The impact of Christian tenets and modern science upon modern life are endless. Modern Western medicine took a similar view of the human body as classical physics did of the universe: "physicians" came to understand the human body as the mechanistic operation of inanimate components with little or

---

10.4 This engraving published in 1680 illustrates the human body as if it were the mechanistic operation of inanimate components entirely divorced from human consciousness. This understanding, adopted by Western medicine, mirrored the orthodox Christian belief that God was divorced from the physical world.

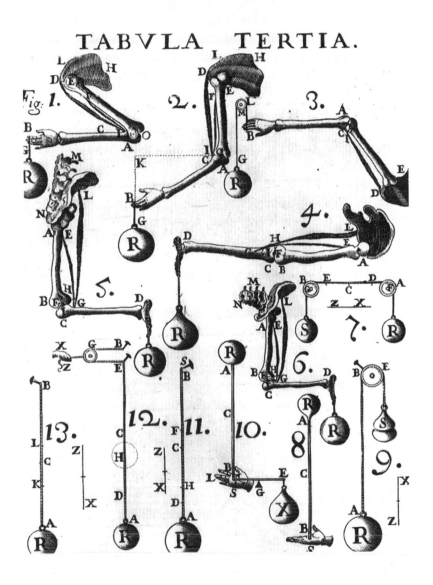

TABVLA TERTIA.

no connection to consciousness. An early proponent of seeing the body as a machine, Thomas Hobbes, wrote in 1651, "For what is the heart, but a spring; and the nerves but so many strings; and the joints, but so many wheels, giving motion to the whole body."[21] As orthodox Christians understood God to be detached from the physical world, so Western medicine understood the workings of the human body to be disconnected from a person's mind or consciousness. Illness was seen simply as a malfunction of mechanical parts, the cause for which lay wholly in the physical world.

In the same way that orthodox Christians tried to subdue lower hierarchical components, Western physicians attempted to prevail over the body rather than to work together with it, by encouraging its ability to heal itself. An example of such a practice is the treatment of non-life-threatening illness with antibiotics. Antibiotics subdue the body's immune system, the body's own capacity to defend itself from illness. While antibiotics are extraordinarily valuable in the treatment of life-threatening illness, the frequent use of them in less serious situations has led to a whole new group of diseases and has spawned new strains of bacteria which do not respond to any known treatment. Many are now calling into question modern medicine's precept that the body is a mechanical instrument devoid of any connection to consciousness, an instrument that is best subdued.

Orthodox Christian ideology has also influenced modern commerce and industry. In mimicry of religious hierarchy, businesses were structured with power vested in a single authority at the top of the organization. Fear, domination and competition, thought so essential to maintain the divine hierarchical order, were seen as necessary characteristics of business. As uniformity was thought to produce unity, so businesses valued conformity and comprised themselves of people of similar race, gender and creed.

More recently, however, a number of companies are finding a different structure and ideology to be more profitable. Businesses in which the employees are valued and are empowered with ownership and responsibility often function more productively than those which adhere to a strict hierarchical model. Cooperation both within a company as well as with its outside suppliers is proving to be more profitable than the fierce competition previously prized. In addition, some are questioning the value of uniformity and sameness in the workplace. An environment in which people have dissimilar perspectives and different ways of solving problems is more likely to produce creative solutions than one in which everyone thinks the same way.

Beyond affecting science, philosophy, medicine and business, orthodox Christianity has had tremendous impact upon modern social structure and government. The belief in singular supremacy, hierarchy, and an inherently sinful human nature thwarts efforts to create pluralistic societies which value individual self-determination. Power and authority within such a belief structure must descend from a singular pinnacle rather than rise from a pluralistic root. Anything that empowers the individual ultimately challenges such an authoritarian structure.

It was, for example, never the intention of New England Puritan leaders to establish a government which represented the people's own views and desires.[22] "Democracy, I do not conceyve, that ever God did ordeyne as a fitt government eyther for church or commonwealth," wrote the Puritan John Cotton. "If the People be governors, who shall be governed?"[23] As the historians Joseph Gaer and Ben Siegel write:

> The Puritans had derived the belief that government's prime function is 'to regulate man's corruption,' that its divinely appointed leaders are to be obeyed unquestioningly, and that the

state's welfare is much more important than the individuals.[24]
The democratic principles established in the United States were created in spite of orthodox Christianity, not because of it. As a treaty written during George Washington's administration and ratified by the U.S. Senate in 1797 stated, "The government of the United States is not, in any sense, founded on the Christian religion."[25]

Orthodox Christians repeatedly opposed religious freedom in America. The Puritan John Norton expressed the orthodox view of liberty of worship as "a liberty to blaspheme, a liberty to seduce others from the true God. A liberty to tell lies in the name of the Lord." When Vermont passed a bill allowing religious liberty, the *Dartmouth Gazette* (November 18, 1807) echoed the orthodox sentiment, calling the bill a striking example "of the pernicious and direful, the infernal consequences to which the leveling spirit of democracy must inevitably tend."[26] During Thomas Jefferson's and James Madison's efforts to separate church and state, Madison pointed to history and argued that whenever "ecclesiastical establishments" had shaped civil society, they had supported political tyranny; never had they protected the people's liberties.[27]

Organized Catholics have done no more than Protestants to support personal liberty and democracy. From opposing the Magna Carta in the thirteenth century, to establishing a precedent for totalitarian states with the Inquisition, to refusing to protest

---

10.5   While some Americans felt the threat to the principles of their Constitution posed by the Roman Catholic Church (as illustrated by this 1855 engraving), fewer were aware of the similar threat posed by the branches of Protestantism. In forging the Constitution and its Bill of Rights, the founding fathers of the United States rejected orthodox Christian ideology. As the U.S. Senate ratified in 1797, "The government of the United States is not, in any sense, founded on the Christian religion."[28]

the attempted Nazi extermination of Jews during World War II,[29] the Catholic Church has championed authoritarianism and opposed democracy and freedom. As the nineteenth century Pope Gregory XVI wrote:

> It is in no way lawful to demand, to defend, or
> to grant unconditional freedom of thought, or
> speech, of writing, or of religion, as if they were
> so many rights that nature has given to man.[30]

Power and authority should, in the eyes of the orthodox, be exercised only by those at the top of the hierarchy.

Orthodox Christianity provided the ideological foundation for modern science and society. Once people had accepted the idea that God was in heaven and not on earth, that there was no more supernatural intervention or magic, scientists and philosophers began to verify just such a world. Their science and philosophy confirmed that the physical world functioned mechanically and independently of consciousness and God. They also corroborated the orthodox Christian belief in the necessity for struggle and domination. These beliefs and concepts, however, are now being called into question, not only because of their practical drawbacks, but also because of their limited scientific accuracy.

&a &a &a

Chapter Eleven

Conclusion

The dark side of Christian history has been and continues to be about the domination and control of spirituality and human freedom. Orthodox Christians built an organization that from its inception encouraged not freedom and self-determination, but obedience and conformity. To that end, any means were justified. Grounded in the belief in a singular, authoritarian and punishing God, orthodox Christians created a church that demanded singular authority and punished those who disobeyed.

During the Dark Ages, civilization collapsed as the Church took control of education, science, medicine, technology and the arts. Crusaders marched into the Middle East killing and destroying in the name of the one Christian God. The Inquisition established a precedent in the Middle Ages for the systematic policing and terrorization of society. The Protestant and Catholic Counter Reformation sparked wars where Christians slaughtered other Christians, each convinced that theirs was the one and only true path. And the holocaust of the witch hunts plumbed the depths of horror as it eradicated countless women and men as well as the belief in earth-based divinity. In 1785 Thomas Jefferson wrote:

> *Millions of innocent men, women, and children, since the introduction of Christianity, have been burnt, tortured, fined, imprisoned; yet we have not advanced one inch towards uniformity. What*

has been the effect of coercion? To make one
half of the world fools, and the other half hypo-
crites. To support error and roguery all over the
earth.[1]

Christianity's impact has been perhaps most insidious upon
the modern world. By terrifying people into believing that there
was no divine supernatural assistance in the physical world,
orthodox Christians created the environment where people
believed the universe to be, pre-determined, mechanical, and
devoid of consciousness. But instead of attributing such an
understanding to religious belief, people now credited science as
having objectively proven such a world. Most people came to
think that struggle, domination and authoritarian control were—
perhaps not divinely ordained—but natural and necessary
qualities of life in such an impersonal universe. Interestingly, the
very science that once verified orthodox Christian concepts is
now discovering the limitations of a mechanistic view of the
universe.

Ignoring the dark side of Christian history perpetuates the
idea that oppression and atrocity are the inevitable results of an
inherently evil or savage human nature. There have been—
especially during the neolithic age—peaceful cultures and
civilizations, however, which functioned without oppressive
hierarchical structures. It is clearly not human nature that causes
people to hurt one another. People of gentler cultures share the
same human nature as we of Western civilization; it is our
beliefs that differ. Tolerant and more peaceful cultures have
respected both masculine and feminine faces of God, both
heavenly and earthly representations of divinity. It is the limited
belief in a singular supremacy and only one face of God that has
resulted in tyranny and brutality.

Ignoring the dark side of Christian history allows the beliefs
which have motivated cruelty to go unexamined. The belief in a
singular face of God who reigns at the pinnacle of a hierarchy

sustained by fear has devastating consequences. People must constantly determine who is superior to whom. Every aspect which differentiates people whether it be gender, race, belief, sexual preference, or socio-economic status, becomes a criterion by which to rank an individual as either better than or less than another. And it is the ranking and subordination of a person's humanity and value that comprises sexism, racism, and the intolerance of difference.

Unity and oneness within an orthodox Christian belief system are perceived to come from sameness and conformity, not from the synergy and harmony of difference. A society's diversity is most often understood to be a liability rather than an asset. A peaceful society is thought to be one where everyone is the same. Within such a belief system, an end to sexism or racism is misunderstood to mean simply a change of roles. Instead of men dominating women, women would dominate men. Instead of whites dominating blacks, blacks would dominate whites. There is no understanding of shared authority, cooperation and support.

Belief in a strictly heavenly or sky-based God who is disconnected from the earth has had enormous ramifications upon humanity's treatment of the natural environment. As orthodox Christianity spread, the means of integrating human activity with seasonal cycles through festivals were curtailed. Holidays came to commemorate biblical events, not the phases of the year. The concept of linear time replaced that of cyclical time, further alienating people from nature's ebb and flow. Modern science then validated the orthodox perception that the earth lacked sanctity by portraying the physical world as a mechanistic realm entirely devoid of consciousness.

However, as dark as moments of Christian history have been, awareness of them need not lead to a complete rejection of Christianity. There have been Christians throughout its history who have fought against the tyranny of orthodox beliefs and behavior. There have been countless Christians who valued love and forgiveness over fear and punishment, who encouraged personal empowerment and understanding over submission and blind faith.

The dark side of Christian history was not an unavoidable result of human nature; it was the result of a very specific ideology and belief structure. As we have ignored the horror of Christian history, so we have ignored scrutiny of Christian beliefs and their pervasiveness in our seemingly godless modern world. Without scrutiny, the destructive patterns have continued to alienate people from God, the natural environment, and each other.

Yet, with understanding and attention, we can stop such harmful patterns. We can recognize that efforts to convince us that God demands our fear and unquestioning submission are in fact efforts to control us and to contain our spirituality. We can recognize that the belief in a singular supremacy lies at the root of chauvinism, racism and totalitarianism. We can move towards a world that values diversity, freedom and human dignity. And we can embrace the hope and pursue the dream that humanity can be free to act humanely.

ﮬ ﮬ ﮬ

Notes

Preface

1. Peggy Polk, "Papal State" (*Chicago Tribune*, June 5, 1995, "Tempo" p. 2.)
2. Ibid., 2.

Chapter One - Seeds of Tyranny

1. Ecclesiastes 12:13.
2. Psalms 128.
3. Luke 12:5.
4. *Tertullianus against Marcion*, Book I, Ch. XXVII. *Ante-Nicene Christian Library* (Edinburgh: T&T Clark)
5. Elaine Pagels, *Adam, Eve and the Serpent* (New York: Random House, 1988) 92.
6. *Tertullianus against Marcion*, Book I, Ch. XXVI.
7. Elaine Pagels, *The Gnostic Gospels* (New York: Random House, 1979) 28.
8. Ibid., 35.
9. Ignatius, *Magnesians* VI and *Trallians* III. *Ante-Nicene Christian Library* (Edinburgh: T&T Clark)
10. "Tripartite Tractate" I,5 79.21-32 from *The Nag Hammadi Library*, James M. Robinson, Director (New York: Harper & Row, 1977) 69.
11. Pagels, *The Gnostic Gospels*, 50.
12. *The Secret Teachings of Jesus*, translated by Marvin W. Meyer (New York: Random House, 1984) 56.
13. *The Excerpta Ex Theodoto of Clement of Alexandria*, translated by Robert Pierce Casey (London: Christophers, 1934) 59.
14. *Irenaeus Against Heresies*, 4.33.3.
15. Ignatius, *Magnesians* VI and *Trallians* III.
16. Pagels, *The Gnostic Gospels*, 42-43.
17. Ibid., 42.
18. Pagels, *Adam, Eve and the Serpent*, 113-114.
19. I Corinthians 11:8 9.
20. Riane Eisler, *The Chalice and the Blade* (San Francisco: Harper & Row, 1987) 131-132.
21. I Timothy 2:11-13.
22. Riane Eisler, *The Chalice and the Blade*, 132-133.

23. *The Essene Gospel of Peace*, edited and translated by Edmond Bordeaux Szekely (San Diego: Academy of Creative Living, 1971) 7.

24. "On the Origin of the World" II.116.2-8 from *The Nag Hammadi Library*, 172.

25. Tertullian, "On Prescription Against Heretics" Chapter XLI, *Ante-Nicene Fathers; Translations of the Writings of the Fathers down to A.A. 325*, Vol. III (Grand Rapids: Wm. B. Eerdmans Publishing Company, 1951) 263.

26. Tertullian, "On the Flesh of Christ" Chapter V, Ibid., 525.

27. Pagels, *The Gnostic Gospels*, 10 and Hans von Campenhausen *Ecclesiastical Authority and Spiritual Power: In the Church of the First Three Centuries*, Translated by J.A. Baker (Stanford University Press, 1969) 18-24.

28. *Irenaeus Against Heresies*, 4.26.2. Volume I (Buffalo: The Christian Literature Publishing Co., 1885)

29. Pagels, *The Gnostic Gospels*, 11.

30. Ibid., 11.

31. Mark 16:9, John 20:11-17.

32. John 20:17.

33. Pagels, *The Gnostic Gospels*, 3-17.

34. *Irenaeus Against Heresies*, 2.27.1-2.

35. Ibid., 2.27.2.

36. Tertullian, "On Prescription Against Heretics" Chapter VII, 246.

37. Ibid., Chapter XIII, 249.

38. Ibid., Chapter XXXVII, 261.

39. Pagels, *The Gnostic Gospels*, xix-xx.

40. *Hippolytus Philosophumena* 6.9, Volume II, Translated by F. Legge (London: Society For Promoting Christian Knowledge, 1921) 5.

41. "Authoritative Teaching" VI, 3 34.32-35.2 from *The Nag Hammadi Library*, 283.

42. Pagels, *The Gnostic Gospels*, 126.

43. "The Gospel of Truth" 29.2-6 from *The Nag Hammadi Library*, 43.

44. "The Gospel of Truth" 17.10-15 from *The Nag Hammadi Library*, 40.

45. Matthew 7:7 and Luke 17:21.

46. Pagels, *The Gnostic Gospels*, 25.

47. Ibid., xxiii.

48. *Irenaeus Against Heresies*, 3.4.1.

49. Ignatius, *Ephesians* V.

50. Pagels, *The Gnostic Gospels*, 34.

Chapter Two - Political Maneuvering

1. Elaine Pagels, *The Gnostic Gospels* (New York: Random House, 1979) 100.

2. John Holland Smith, *The Death of Classical Paganism*, (New York: Charles Scribner, 1976) 49.

3. *St. Irenaeus, Proof of the Apostolic Preaching*, translated and annotated by Josephy P. Smith (Westminster, Maryland: The Newman Press, 1952) 106.

4.   Smith, *The Death of Classical Paganism*, 5.
5.   Pagels, *The Gnostic Gospels*, 21.
6.   Joel Carmichael, *The Birth of Christianity* (New York: Hippocrene Books, 1989) 170-171.
7.   Pagels, *The Gnostic Gospels*, 104.
8.   Ibid., 104.
9.   Michael Baigent, Richard Leigh & Henry Lincoln, *Holy Blood, Holy Grail* (New York: Dell, 1982) 364, 318.
10.   Barbara Walker, *The Woman's Encyclopedia of Myths and Secrets* (San Francisco: Harper & Row, 1983) 467.
11.   Ibid., 469.
12.   Lloyd M. Graham, *Deceptions and Myths of the Bible* (New York: Citadel Press, 1975) 445.
13.   Ibid., 445.
14.   Baigent, Leigh, Lincoln, *Holy Blood, Holy Grail*, 327-329.
15.   Ibid., 317-318.
16.   Ibid., 317.
17.   Riane Eisler, *The Chalice and the Blade* (San Francisco: Harper & Row, 1987) 131.
18.   Luke 23:2.
19.   Baigent, Leigh, Lincoln, *Holy Blood, Holy Grail*, 326-327.
20.   Carmichael, *The Birth of Christianity*, 35, 177, 178.
21.   See both *Holy Blood, Holy Grail* and Joel Carmichael's *The Birth of Christianity* for further discussion.
22.   Walter Nigg, *The Heretics: Heresy Through the Ages*, Edited and translated by Richard and Clara Winston (New York: Dorset Press, 1962) 127. The quoted material is by E. Schwarz and is taken from the same page of text.
23.   *The Secret Teachings of Jesus*, translated by Marvin W. Meyer (New York: Random House, 1984) 56.
24.   "The Sophia of Jesus Christ" III,4, from *The Nag Hammadi Library* edited by James M. Robinson (New York: Harper & Row, 1977) 217.
25.   Geoffrey Ashe, *The Virgin: Mary's Cult and the Re-emergence of the Goddess* (London: Arkana, 1976, 1988) 206.
26.   Pagels, *The Gnostic Gospels*, 52.
27.   Francis X. Weiser, *Handbook of Christian Feasts and Customs* (New York: Harcourt, Brace & Co., 1952) 257.
28.   Robert W. Ackerman, *Backgrounds to Medieval English Literature* (New York: Random House, 1966) 92.
29.   Ashe, *The Virgin*, 224-225.
30.   Walker, *The Woman's Encyclopedia of Myths and Secrets*, 663.
31.   Arthur Cotterell, *Myths and Legends* (New York: MacMillan Publishing Company, 1989) 131.
32.   Walker, *The Woman's Encyclopedia of Myths and Secrets*, 663-665.
33.   Sir James George Frazer, *The Golden Bough* Vol.1 abridged edition (New York: Collier Books, 1922) 415.

34.   Ashe, *The Virgin*, 179.
35.   Ibid., 8, 125.
36.   Ibid., 139, 150-151.
37.   Walker, *The Woman's Encyclopedia of Myths and Secrets*, 611.
38.   Ashe, *The Virgin*, 129.
39.   Ibid., 151.
40.   Ibid., 191.
41.   Ibid., 192.
42.   Ibid., 192-193.
43.   Charles Merrill Smith, *The Pearly Gates Syndicate* (New York: DoubleDay, 1971) 27-28.
44.   J.N. Hillgarth, *The Conversion of Western Europe* (Englewood Cliffs, NJ: Prentice Hall, 1969) 49.
45.   Ibid., 46.
46.   Smith, *The Death of Classical Paganism*, 218.
47.   Ibid., 166-167.
48.   Hillgarth, *The Conversion of Western Europe*, 44-48.

Chapter Three - Deciding Upon Doctrine

1.   Evrett Ferguson, Michael P. McHugh & Frederick W. Norris, *Encyclopedia of Early Christianity* (New York & London: Garland Publishing, 1990) 420.
2.   Walter Nigg, *The Heretics: Heresy Through the Ages* (New York: Dorset Press, 1962) 138.
3.   Ibid., 138.
4.   Elaine Pagels, *Adam, Eve and the Serpent* (New York: Random House, 1988) 107.
5.   Saint Augustine, *The City of God*, Book XIV, Ch.4, translated by Marcus Dods (New York: The Modern Library, 1950) 445.
6.   Pagels, *Adam, Eve and the Serpent*, 141.
7.   Augustine, *The City of God*, Book XIV, Ch. 16, 465.
8.   Pagels, *Adam, Eve and the Serpent*, 131-134.
9.   Nigg, *The Heretics*, 37.
10.   Barbara Walker, *The Woman's Encyclopedia of Myths and Secrets* (San Francisco: Harper & Row, 1983) 910.
11.   Pagels, *Adam, Eve and the Serpent*, 28.
12.   Ibid., 45.
13.   Ibid., 107.
14.   Augustine, *The City of God*, Book XIV, Ch. 15, 462.
15.   Pagels, *Adam, Eve and the Serpent*, 125.
16.   Ibid., 129-130, 134.
17.   Quincy Howe, Jr., *Reincarnation For The Christian* (Philadelphia: Westminster Press, 1974) 65-72.
18.   Ibid., 66.
19.   *Reincarnation*, compiled and edited by Joseph Head and S.L. Cranston (New

York: The Julian Press, 1961) 38.
20. Howe, *Reincarnation For The Christian*, 81.
21. Ibid., 67.
22. *The New Columbia Encyclopedia* edited by William H. Harris and Judith S. Levey (New York & London: Columbia University Press, 1975) 782.
23. Nigg, *The Heretics*, 117.
24. Ibid., 116.
25. Lloyd M. Graham, *Deceptions and Myths of the Bible* (New York: Citadel Press, 1975) 468.
26. Keith Thomas, *Religion and the Decline of Magic* (New York: Charles Scribner's Sons, 1974) 477.

Chapter Four - The Church Takes Over

1. Charles Panati, *Panati's Extraordinary Endings of Practically Everything* (New York: Harper & Row, 1989) 225-228.
2. Ibid., 225.
3. Ibid., 225.
4. Ibid., 264-265.
5. Charles Panati, *Extraordinary Origins of Everyday Things* (New York: Harper & Row, 1987) 201-202.
6. Ibid., 131.
7. Ibid., 328.
8. *The New Columbia Encyclopedia* edited by William H. Harris and Judith S. Levey (New York & London: Columbia University Press, 1975) 2331.
9. Lloyd M. Graham, *Deceptions and Myths of the Bible* (New York: Citadel Press, 1975) 448.
10. Ibid., 449.
11. Daniel J. Boorstin, *The Discoverers* (New York: Random House, 1983) 573.
12. Ibid., 572.
13. Ibid., 573.
14. Ibid., 573.
15. Riane Eisler, *The Chalice and the Blade* (San Francisco: Harper & Row, 1987) and Merlin Stone, *When God Was a Woman* (New York: Dorset Press, 1976).
16. Boorstin, *The Discoverers*, 573.
17. *The New Columbia Encyclopedia*, 61, and Eisler, *The Chalice and the Blade*.
18. Graham, *Deceptions and Myths of the Bible*, 444.
19. Jeffrey Burton Russell, *A History of Medieval Christianity* (New York: Thomas Y. Cromwell, 1968) 103.
20. Ibid., 40.
21. Charles Homer Haskins, *The Renaissance of the 12th Century* (Cleveland & New York: Meridian Books, 1927) 96.
22. Barbara G. Walker, *The Woman's Encyclopedia of Myths and Secrets* (San Francisco: Harper & Row, 1983) 208.

23.   Haskins, *The Renaissance of the 12th Century*, 95.
24.   John H. Smith, *The Death of Classical Paganism* (New York: Charles Scribner's Sons, 1976) 223.
25.   Walker, *The Woman's Encyclopedia of Myths and Secrets*, 208.
26.   Smith, *The Death of Classical Paganism*, 247.
27.   Haskins, *The Renaissance of the 12th Century*, 34.
28.   Ibid., 43.
29.   Boorstin, *The Discoverers*, 581.
30.   H. Daniel-Rops, *Cathedral and Crusade* (New York: E.P.Dutton & Company, Inc., 1957) 273.
31.   Ibid., 274.
32.   Malachi Martin, *Decline and Fall of the Roman Church* (New York: G.P. Putnam's Sons, 1981) 141.
33.   Graham, *Deceptions and Myths of the Bible*, 464.
34.   Russell, *A History of Medieval Christianity*, 92, and Graham, *Deceptions and Myths of the Bible*, 470.
35.   Russell, *A History of Medieval Christianity*, 92.
36.   Ibid., 65.
37.   Ibid., 93.
38.   Joan O'Grady, *The Prince of Darkness* (Longmead: Element Books, 1989) 62.
39.   Smith, *The Death of Classical Paganism*, 229.
40.   Ibid., 246.

Chapter Five - The Church Fights Change

1.   Jeffrey Burton Russell, *A History of Medieval Christianity* (New York: Thomas Y. Cromwell, 1968) 106.
2.   Charles Homer Haskins, *The Renaissance of the 12th Century* (Cleveland & New York: Meridian Books, 1927) 62.
3.   Albert Clement Shannon, *The Medieval Inquisition* (Washington D.C.: Augustinian College Press, 1983) 141.
4.   Ibid., 141.
5.   Haskins, *The Renaissance of the 12th Century*, 45.
6.   Ibid., 364.
7.   Walter Nigg, *The Heretics: Heresy Through the Ages* (New York: Dorset Press, 1962) 169.
8.   Haskins, *The Renaissance of the 12th Century*, 96.
9.   Ibid., 97.
10.   Ibid., 55-56.
11.   Jacob Burckhardt, *The Civilization of the Renaissance in Italy*, edited by Irene Gordon (New York: Mentor Books, 1960) 336.
12.   Russell, *A History of Medieval Christianity*, 97-98.
13.   Barbara W. Tuchman, *A Distant Mirror* (New York: Ballantine Books, 1978) 327.

14. Henri Daniel-Rops, *Cathedral and Crusade* (New York: E.P. Dutton & Company, Inc., 1957) 246.

15. Henry C. Lea, *History of Sacerdotal Celibacy in the Christian Church*, 4th edition revised (London: Watts & Co., 1932) 264, 279.

16. Barbara G. Walker, *The Woman's Encyclopedia of Myths and Secrets* (San Francisco: Harper & Row, 1983) 438.

17. Daniel-Rops, *Cathedral and Crusade*, 521.

18. Theodore Nottingham, "The Birth Within: Meister Eckhart and the Knowing of God" *GNOSIS*, No.18 (Winter 1991) 19.

19. Walker, *The Woman's Encyclopedia of Myths and Secrets*, 212.

20. Jeffrey Burton Russell, *Witchcraft in the Middle Ages* (Ithaca & London: Cornell University Press, 1972) 102.

21. Geoffrey Ashe, *The Virgin: Mary's Cult and the Re-emergence of the Goddess* (London: Arkana, 1976, 1988) 219.

22. Ibid., 217.

23. Ibid., 217, 221.

24. Ibid., 154.

25. Russell, *A History of Medieval Christianity*, 124-126, 150.

26. Russell, *A History of Medieval Christianity*, 149, and Haskins, *The Renaissance of the 12th Century*, 207.

27. Henry Charles Lea, *The Inquisition of the Middle Ages*, Abridgement by Margaret Nicholson (New York: MacMillan, 1961) 24.

28. Haskins, *The Renaissance of the 12th Century*, 217-218.

29. Daniel-Rops, *Cathedral and Crusade*, 240.

30. Ibid., 241.

31. Russell, *A History of Medieval Christianity*, 165.

32. Ibid., 75.

33. Lloyd M. Graham, *Deceptions and Myths of the Bible* (New York: Citadel Press, 1975) 470.

34. Ibid., 470.

35. Phillip Schaff, *History of the Christian Church* Vol. V: The Middle Ages (Grand Rapids, MI: Wm. B. Eerdmans, 1952) 775-6.

36. Russell, *A History of Medieval Christianity*, 168-169.

37. Daniel-Rops, *Cathedral and Crusade*, 433-435.

38. Malachi Martin, *Decline and Fall of the Roman Church* (New York: G.P. Putnam's Sons, 1981) 134, and Daniel-Rops, *Cathedral and Crusade*, 276.

39. James A. Haught, *Holy Horrors* (Buffalo: Prometheus, 1990) 25-26.

40. Martin, *Decline and Fall of the Roman Church*, 134.

41. Haskins, *The Renaissance of the 12th Century*, 280.

42. Russell, *A History of Medieval Christianity*, 75.

43. Ibid., 64.

44. Daniel-Rops, *Cathedral and Crusade*, 439-441.

45. G.G. Coulton, *Inquisition and Liberty* (Glouster, MA: Peter Smith, 1969) 165.

46. Russell, *A History of Medieval Christianity*, 159-160.

47.   Karen Armstrong, *Holy War: The Crusades and Their Impact on Today's World* (New York: Doubleday, 1988) 387.
48.   Coulton, *Inquisition and Liberty*, 164-165.
49.   Luke 19:27.
50.   Martin, *Decline and Fall of the Roman Church*, 134.
51.   The common belief that the crusaders returned from their exploits with literature and learning is mistaken. To quote Charles H. Haskins, "The Crusaders were men of action, not men of learning, and little can be traced in the way of translations in Palestine or Syria." (*The Renaissance of the 12th Century*, 282.)
52.   Graham, *Deceptions and Myths of the Bible*, 444.
53.   For more discussion, see Karen Armstrong, *Holy War: The Crusades and Their Impact on Today's World.*
54.   Russell, *A History of Medieval Christianity*, 75.
55.   Ibid., 156.
56.   Ibid., 155.
57.   Ibid., 157.
58.   Walker, *The Woman's Encyclopedia of Myths and Secrets*, 510.
59.   Ibid., 510.
60.   Martin, *Decline and Fall of the Roman Church*, 146.
61.   Tuchman, *A Distant Mirror*, 321-322.
62.   Ibid., 322.
63.   *The New Columbia Encyclopedia* edited by William H. Harris and Judith S. Levey (New York & London: Columbia University Press, 1975) 2442.
64.   Coulton, *Inquisition and Liberty*, 59.
65.   Lea, *The Inquisition of the Middle Ages*, 27.
66.   Timothy O'Neill, "Century of Marvels, Century of Light" 14-18 and Judith Mann, "The Legend of the Cathars" *GNOSIS*, No.4, 28.
67.   Ian Begg, *The Cult of the Black Virgin* (London: Arkana, 1985) 136 and Lea, *The Inquisition of the Middle Ages*, 43.
68.   Otto Rahn, *Kreuzzug gegen den Gral*, as quoted in Nigg, *The Heretics*, 182-183.
69.   Lea, *The Inquisition of the Middle Ages*, 74.
70.   Russell, *Witchcraft in the Middle Ages*, 125.
71.   Lea, *The Inquisition of the Middle Ages*, 46.
72.   Ibid., 54.
73.   Ibid., 54.
74.   Ibid., 57-59.
75.   Ibid., 64.
76.   John Kimsey, "The Code of Love," *GNOSIS*, No.18 (Winter 1991) 27.
77.   Lea, *The Inquisition of the Middle Ages*, 75.
78.   Friedrich Heer, *The Medieval World*, translated by Janet Sondheimer, (New York: NAL, 1961) 214.
79.   Lea, *The Inquisition of the Middle Ages*, 75.

Chapter Six - Controlling the Human Spirit

1. Henry Kamen, *Inquisition and Society in Spain* (Bloomington: Indiana University Press, 1985) 161.
2. G.G. Coulton, *Inquisition and Liberty* (Glouster, MA: Peter Smith, 1969) 81.
3 Peter Tompkins, "Symbols of Heresy" in *The Magic of Obelisks* (New York: Harper, 1981) 57.
4. Henry Charles Lea, *The Inquisition of the Middle Ages*, Abridgement by Margaret Nicholson (New York: MacMillan, 1961) 221-222.
5. Henri Daniel-Rops, *Cathedral and Crusade* (New York: E.P.Dutton & Company, Inc., 1957) 547 and Jeffrey Burton Russell, *Witchcraft in the Middle Ages* (Ithaca & London: Cornell University Press, 1972) 155.
6. Rossell Hope Robbins, *The Encyclopedia of Witchcraft and Demonology* (New York: Bonanza Books, 1981) 13.
7. Lea, *The Inquisition of the Middle Ages*, 216.
8. Ibid., 211.
9. Ibid., 214.
10. Ibid., 215.
11. Ibid., 214.
12. Ibid., 177-179.
13. Ibid., 177.
14. Ibid., 174.
15. Ibid., 226-227.
16. Coulton, *Inquisition and Liberty*, 132.
17. Barbara G. Walker, *The Woman's Encyclopedia of Myths and Secrets* (San Francisco: Harper & Row, 1983) 439.
18. Lea, *The Inquisition of the Middle Ages*, 248.
19. Ibid., 226-227.
20. Robbins, *The Encyclopedia of Witchcraft and Demonology*, 271.
21. Ibid., 271.
22. Barbara W. Tuchman, *A Distant Mirror* (New York: Ballantine Books, 1978) 36.
23. Walker, *The Woman's Encyclopedia of Myths and Secrets*, 438.
24. Daniel J. Boorstin, *The Discoverers* (New York: Random House, 1983) 275.
25. Lea, *The Inquisition of the Middle Ages*, 70.
26. Ibid., 248.
27. Ibid., 232-233.
28. Ibid., 222.
29. Ibid., 224-225.
30. Ibid., 233-236.
31. Walter Nigg, *The Heretics: Heresy Through the Ages* (New York: Dorset Press, 1962) 220.
32. John 15:16.
33. Walker, *The Woman's Encyclopedia of Myths and Secrets*, 443.
34. Lea, *The Inquisition of the Middle Ages*, 252.

35. Coulton, *Inquisition and Liberty*, 154-155.
36. Ibid., 148.
37. Jean Plaidy, *The Spanish Inquisition* (New York: Citadel Press, 1967) 139.
38. Coulton, *Inquisition and Liberty*, 154-155.
39. Walker, *The Woman's Encyclopedia of Myths and Secrets*, 1007.
40. Coulton, *Inquisition and Liberty*, 155.
41. Walker, *The Woman's Encyclopedia of Myths and Secrets*, 445.
42. Plaidy, *The Spanish Inquisition*, 138-145.
43. Coulton, *Inquisition and Liberty*, 169.
44. Kamen, *Inquisition and Society in Spain*, 163.
45. Ibid., 164.
46. John Bossy, *Christianity in the West 1400-1700* (Oxford: Oxford University Press, 1985) 84-85.
47. Jeffrey Burton Russell, *A History of Medieval Christianity* (New York: Thomas Y. Cromwell, 1968) 157.
48. Kamen, *Inquisition and Society in Spain*, 161.
49. Walker, *The Woman's Encyclopedia of Myths and Secrets*, 472.
50. Kamen, *Inquisition and Society in Spain*, 14-29.
51. Hugh A. Mulligan, "Columbus Saga Sinking Fast" (Associated Press, March 8, 1992).
52. Jon Margolis, "War of words over Columbus rages on", *The Sunday Denver Post*, July 28, 1991, p.7.
53. Ibid., 7,20.
54. Cecil Roth, *The Spanish Inquisition* (New York: W. W. Norton & Company, 1964) 210.
55. Plaidy, *The Spanish Inquisition*, 165.
56. Roth, *The Spanish Inquisition*, 221.
57. Jean Delumeau, *Catholicism Between Luther and Voltaire* (London: Burns and Oats, 1977) 90.
58. Walker, *The Woman's Encyclopedia of Myths and Secrets*, 447.
59. Delumeau, *Catholicism Between Luther and Voltaire*, 79.
60. "Tripartite Tractate" I,5 - 79.21-32 from *The Nag Hammadi Library*, James M. Robinson, Director (New York: Harper & Row, 1977) 69.
61. Delumeau, *Catholicism Between Luther and Voltaire*, 82.
62. Forrest Wood, *The Arrogance of Faith* (New York: Alfred A. Knopf, 1990) 13.
63. Delumeau, *Catholicism Between Luther and Voltaire*, 82.
64. Ibid., 85.
65. Ibid., 85.
66. Leviticus 25:44-46.
67. Ephesians 6:5, I Timothy 6:1, Titus 2:9-10.
68. Daniel-Rops, *Cathedral and Crusade*, 263.
69. Elaine Pagels, *Adam, Eve and the Serpent* (New York: Random House, 1988) 114.
70. Delumeau, *Catholicism Between Luther and Voltaire*, 88.

71.   Wood, *The Arrogance of Faith*, 119.
72.   Ibid., 127.
73.   Walker, *The Woman's Encyclopedia of Myths and Secrets*, 447.

Chapter Seven - The Reformation

1.   Lloyd M. Graham, *Deceptions and Myths of the Bible* (New York: Citadel Press, 1975) 461.
2.   John Bossy, *Christianity in the West 1400-1700* (Oxford: Oxford University Press, 1985) 97.
3.   Ibid., 94, 109.
4.   Ibid., 95.
5.   Ibid., 28.
6.   Jean Delumeau, *Catholicism Between Luther and Voltaire* (London: Burns and Oats, 1977) 9.
7.   Keith Thomas, *Religion and the Decline of Magic* (New York: Charles Scribner's Sons, 1974) 56.
8.   Delumeau, *Catholicism Between Luther and Voltaire*, 10.
9.   Ibid., 15.
10.   *The "Natural Inferiority" of Women* compiled by Tama Starr (New York: Poseidon Press, 1991) 36.
11.   *The New Columbia Encyclopedia* edited by William H. Harris and Judith S. Levey (New York & London: Columbia University Press, 1975) 1631.
12.   Bossy, *Christianity in the West 1400-1700*, 86.
13.   Walter Nigg, *The Heretics: Heresy Through the Ages* (New York: Dorset Press, 1962) 304-305 and James A. Haught, *Holy Horrors* (Buffalo: Prometheus, 1990) 111.
14.   Jean Delumeau, *Sin and Fear*, translated by Eric Nicholson (New York: St. Martins Press, 1990) 536.
15.   Brian P. Levack, *The Witch-Hunt in Early Modern Europe* (London: Longman, 1987) 103.
16.   Bossy, *Christianity in the West 1400-1700*, 59-62.
17.   Bossy, *Christianity in the West 1400-1700*, 47, 134, and Thomas, *Religion and the Decline of Magic*, 155.
18.   Bossy, *Christianity in the West 1400-1700*, 117-118.
19.   Ibid., 35, 116.
20.   Joseph Gaer and Ben Siegel, *The Puritan Heritage: America's Roots in the Bible* (New York: Mentor Books, 1964) 74-76.
21.   Bossy, *Christianity in the West 1400-1700*, 125, 134.
22.   Thomas, *Religion and the Decline of Magic*, 161.
23.   Ibid., 161.
24.   Ibid., 162.
25.   Delumeau, *Catholicism Between Luther and Voltaire*, 44.
26.   Charles Panati, *Extraordinary Origins of Everyday Things* (New York: Harper & Row, 1987) 202.

27. Delumeau, *Sin and Fear*, 437.
28. Ibid., 437.
29. Ibid., 438-439.
30. Heinrich Kramer and James Sprenger, *The Malleus Maleficarum*, Translated by Montague Summers (New York: Dover Publications, 1971) 167.
31. Reay Tannahill, Sex In History (Michigan: Scarborough House, 1992) 161 and Karen Armstrong, *The Gospel According to Woman: Christianity's Creation of the Sex War in the West* (New York: Doubleday, 1986) 329.
32. Delumeau, *Sin and Fear*, 438.
33. Ibid., 438.
34. Gaer and Siegel, *The Puritan Heritage: America's Roots in the Bible*, 87.
35. Ibid., 31.
36. Ibid., 31.
37. Ibid., 88.
38. Ibid., 87.
39. Delumeau, *Catholicism Between Luther and Voltaire*, 43.
40. Delumeau, *Sin and Fear*, 27.
41. Jonathan Edwards, "The Justice of God in the Damnation of Sinners," from *The Works of Jonathan Edwards, A.M.* (London: Henry G. Bohn) 673.
42. Bossy, *Christianity in the West 1400-1700*, 126.
43. Gaer and Siegel, *The Puritan Heritage: America's Roots in the Bible*, 118.
44. Delumeau, *Catholicism Between Luther and Voltaire*, 47.
45. Delumeau, *Sin and Fear*, 457.
46. Thomas, *Religion and the Decline of Magic*, 278.
47. Ibid., 52, 269-270.
48. Ibid., 278.
49. Ibid., 278.
50. Ibid., 277.
51. Bossy, *Christianity in the West 1400-1700*, 68.
52. Thomas, *Religion and the Decline of Magic*, 29, 44.
53. Ibid., 503.
54. Ibid., 53.
55. Ibid., 52.
56. Ibid., 56.
57. Ibid., 57.
58. Delumeau, *Sin and Fear*, 460.
59. Ibid., 461.
60. Levack, *The Witch-Hunt in Early Modern Europe*, 97.
61. Ibid., 97.
62. Ibid., 97.
63. Thomas, *Religion and the Decline of Magic*, 471.
64. Joan O'Grady, *The Prince of Darkness* (Longmead: Element Books, 1989) 110.
65. Thomas, *Religion and the Decline of Magic*, 476.
66. Ibid., 476.

67. Delumeau, *Catholicism Between Luther and Voltaire*, 173.
68. Delumeau, *Sin and Fear*, 496.
69. Thomas, *Religion and the Decline of Magic*, 472.

Chapter Eight - The Witch Hunts

1. Rossell Hope Robbins, *The Encyclopedia of Witchcraft and Demonology* (New York: Bonanza Books, 1981) 3.
2. I Peter 3:7.
3. *The "Natural Inferiority" of Women* compiled by Tama Starr (New York: Poseidon Press, 1991) 45.
4. Joan Smith, *Misogynies: Reflections on Myths and Malice* (New York: Fawcett Columbine, 1989) 66.
5. *The "Natural Inferiority" of Women*, Starr, 45.
6. Karen Armstrong, *The Gospel According to Woman: Christianity's Creation of the Sex War in the West* (New York: Doubleday, 1986) 71.
7. Smith, *Misogynies*, 61.
8. Saint Thomas Aquinas, *Summa Theologica* (New York & London: Blackfriars, McGraw-Hill, Eyre & Spottiswoode) Question 92, 35.
9. Armstrong, *The Gospel According to Woman*, 69.
10. Apocrypha, Ecclesiasticus 25:13-26.
11. Walter Nigg, *The Heretics: Heresy Through the Ages* (New York: Dorset Press, 1962) 277.
12. Keith Thomas, *Religion and the Decline of Magic* (New York: Charles Scribner's Sons, 1974) 520.
13. Carol F. Karlsen, *The Devil in the Shape of a Woman* (Vintage Books: New York, 1987) 266.
14. Barbara W. Tuchman, *A Distant Mirror* (New York: Ballantine Books, 1978) 211.
15. Ibid., 211.
16. Joan O'Grady, *The Prince of Darkness* (Longmead: Element Books, 1989) 84.
17. Henry Kamen, *Inquisition and Society in Spain* (Bloomington: Indiana University Press, 1985) 163.
18. Jean Plaidy, *The Spanish Inquisition* (New York: Citadel Press, 1967) 143.
19. Heinrich Kramer and James Sprenger, *The Malleus Maleficarum*, Translated by Montague Summers (New York: Dover Publications, 1971) 121.
20. Ibid., 121.
21. Thomas, *Religion and the Decline of Magic*, 568-569.
22. *The Merriam-Webster Dictionary* (New York: Pocket Books, 1974) 215.
23. Julio Caro Baroja, *The World of Witches* (Chicago: University of Chicago Press, 1961) 60-61 and Brian P. Levack, *The Witch-Hunt in Early Modern Europe* (London: Longman, 1987) 45.
24. Jeffrey Burton Russell, *Witchcraft in the Middle Ages* (Ithaca & London: Cornell University Press, 1972) 76-77.
25. O'Grady, *The Prince of Darkness*, 62.

26. Baroja, *The World of Witches*, 81.
27. Bengt Ankarloo and Gustav Henningsen, *Early Modern European Witchcraft Centres and Peripheries* (Oxford: Clarendon Press, 1990) 25.
28. Russell, *Witchcraft in the Middle Ages*, 164.
29. Ibid., 134.
30. Margot Adler, *Drawing Down the Moon* (New York: Beacon Press, 1979) 49.
31. Baroja, *The World of Witches*, 149-150.
32. Thomas, *Religion and the Decline of Magic*, 43.
33. Nigg, *The Heretics*, 280 and Jean Delumeau, *Catholicism Between Luther and Voltaire* (London: Burns and Oats, 1977) 174.
34. Delumeau, *Catholicism Between Luther and Voltaire*, 174.
35. Baroja, *The World of Witches*, 165.
36. Ibid., 165.
37. Jeffrey Burton Russell, *A History of Medieval Christianity* (New York: Thomas Y. Cromwell, 1968) 173.
38. Ibid., 173.
39. Levack, *The Witch-Hunt in Early Modern Europe*, 49.
40. Smith, *Misogynies*, 68.
41. Montague Summers, *The History of Witchcraft and Demonology* (New York: New Hyde Park, 1956) 12.
42. Robbins, *The Encyclopedia of Witchcraft and Demonology*, 9.
43. Exodus 22:18.
44. Barbara G. Walker, *The Woman's Encyclopedia of Myths and Secrets* (San Francisco: Harper & Row, 1983) 1088.
45. Ibid., 1088.
46. Summers, *The History of Witchcraft and Demonology*, 63.
47. Robbins, *The Encyclopedia of Witchcraft and Demonology*, 271.
48. Walker, *The Woman's Encyclopedia of Myths and Secrets*, 1086.
49. Robbins, *The Encyclopedia of Witchcraft and Demonology*, 16.
50. Levack, *The Witch-Hunt in Early Modern Europe*, 110.
51. Nigg, *The Heretics*, 281.
52. Baroja, *The World of Witches*, 168-169.
53. Thomas, *Religion and the Decline of Magic*, 502.
54. Walker, *The Woman's Encyclopedia of Myths and Secrets*, 1004.
55. Ibid., 445.
56. Russell, *Witchcraft in the Middle Ages*, 151.
57. Walker, *The Woman's Encyclopedia of Myths and Secrets*, 445-446.
58. Ibid., 445.
59. Ibid., 1004.
60. Robbins, *The Encyclopedia of Witchcraft and Demonology*, 229.
61. Ibid., 4.
62. Levack, *The Witch-Hunt in Early Modern Europe*, 105.
63. Ibid., 59.
64. Ibid., 59.
65. Ibid., 59.

66. Levack, *The Witch-Hunt in Early Modern Europe*, 102, and Thomas, *Religion and the Decline of Magic*, 493-495.

67. Shakespeare, *The Tempest*, epilogue, written in 1610-1611.

68. Levack, *The Witch Hunt in Early Modern Europe*, 149-150.

69. Ibid., 150.

70. Thomas, *Religion and the Decline of Magic*, 551, and Walker, *The Woman's Encyclopedia of Myths and Secrets*, 1008.

71. Walker, *The Woman's Encyclopedia of Myths and Secrets*, 1083.

72. Robbins, *The Encyclopedia of Witchcraft and Demonology*, 4.

73. Thomas, *Religion and the Decline of Magic*, 555.

74. Ibid., 554.

75. Ibid., 436.

76. Ibid., 177.

77. Ibid., 265-266.

78. Ibid., 266.

79. Ibid., 266.

80. Ibid., 178.

81. Ibid., 479.

82. Ibid., 265.

83. Ibid., 479.

84. Ibid., 85.

85. Ibid., 264.

86. Ibid., 264.

87. Jeanne Achterberg, *Woman As Healer* (Boston: Shambala, 1991) 105.

88. Ibid., 106.

89. Thomas, *Religion and the Decline of Magic*, 14.

90. Ibid., 537.

91. Ibid., 537.

92. Robbins, *The Encyclopedia of Witchcraft and Demonology*, 540.

93. Ibid., 540.

94. John T. Noonan, Jr., *Contraception* (New York and Toronto: The New American Library, 1965) 42.

95. Achterberg, *Woman As Healer*, 92.

96. Robbins, *The Encyclopedia of Witchcraft and Demonology*, 540.

97. Baroja, *The World of Witches*, 125.

98. Robbins, *The Encyclopedia of Witchcraft and Demonology*, 4.

99. Walker, *The Woman's Encyclopedia of Myths and Secrets*, 655.

100. Genesis 3:16.

101. Walker, *The Woman's Encyclopedia of Myths and Secrets*, 656.

102. Ibid., 656.

103. Armstrong, *The Gospel According to Woman*, 69.

104. Walker, *The Woman's Encyclopedia of Myths and Secrets*, 444.

105. Ibid., 444.

106. Robbins, *The Encyclopedia of Witchcraft and Demonology*, 4-5.

107. Walker, *The Woman's Encyclopedia of Myths and Secrets*, 1087.

108. Levack, *The Witch-Hunt in Early Modern Europe*, 229.
109. Ibid., 229.
110. Ibid., 229.
111. Robbins, *The Encyclopedia of Witchcraft and Demonology*, 17.
112. Ibid., 17.

Chapter Nine - Alienation from Nature

1. Colossians 3:5-6.
2. James 3:14-15.
3. Philippians 3:18-19.
4. Genesis 3:17-18.
5. Lewis Regenstein, *Replenish the Earth* (New York: Crossroad, 1991) 72.
6. Ibid., 75.
7. Barry Holstun Lopez, *Of Wolves and Men* (New York: Charles Scribner's Sons, 1978) 238-239.
8. Regenstein, *Replenish the Earth*, 73.
9. Ibid., 74-76.
10. Keith Thomas, *Religion and the Decline of Magic* (New York: Charles Scribner's Sons, 1974) 9.
11. John Holland Smith, *The Death of Classical Paganism*, (New York: Charles Scribner, 1976) 240-241.
12. Ibid., 246.
13. William Anderson, *Green Man* (London and San Francisco: Harpercollins, 1990) 51,52-53,50.
14. Ibid., 52.
15. Ibid., 63.
16. Sir James George Frazer, *The Golden Bough* Vol.1 Abridged Edition (New York: Collier Books, 1922) 416.
17. Francis X. Weiser, *Handbook of Christian Feasts and Customs* (New York: Harcourt, Brace & Co., 1952) 53.
18. Jeffrey Burton Russell, *Witchcraft in the Middle Ages* (Ithaca & London: Cornell University Press, 1972) 51.
19. Weiser, *Handbook of Christian Feasts and Customs*, 141.
20. Daniel J. Boorstin, *The Discoverers* (New York: Random House, 1983) 599.
21. Barbara G. Walker, *The Woman's Encyclopedia of Myths and Secrets* (San Francisco: Harper & Row, 1983) 116-118.
22. Frazer, *The Golden Bough*, 419.
23. Weiser, *Handbook of Christian Feasts and Customs*, 215-216.
24. Ibid., 290.
25. Ibid., 291.
26. Ibid., 278, 309.
27. Barbara G. Walker, *The Woman's Dictionary of Symbols and Sacred Objects* (San Francisco: Harper & Row, 1988) 344-345.
28. Jean Delumeau, *Sin and Fear*, translated by Eric Nicholson (New York: St.

Martins Press, 1990) 457.
29.   Anderson, *Green Man*, 31.
30.   Walker, *The Woman's Encyclopedia of Myths and Secrets*, 759.
31.   Jean Delumeau, *Catholicism Between Luther and Voltaire* (London: Burns and Oats, 1977) 177.
32.   Walker, *The Woman's Dictionary of Symbols and Sacred Objects*, 176.
33.   Joseph Gaer and Ben Siegel, *The Puritan Heritage: America's Roots in the Bible* (New York: Mentor Books, 1964) 92.
34.   Delumeau, *Sin and Fear*, 437.
35.   Walker, *The Woman's Dictionary of Symbols and Sacred Objects*, 176.
36.   *The "Natural Inferiority" of Women* compiled by Tama Starr (New York: Poseidon Press, 1991) 46.
37.   Delumeau, *Catholicism Between Luther and Voltaire*, 197.
38.   Thomas, *Religion and the Decline of Magic*, 66.
39.   Gaer and Siegel, *The Puritan Heritage: America's Roots in the Bible*, 86.
40.   Ibid., 86-87.
41.   Ibid., 86.
42.   Weiser, *Handbook of Christian Feasts and Customs*, 64.
43.   Ibid., 65.
44.   Gaer and Siegel, *The Puritan Heritage: America's Roots in the Bible*, 85.
45.   Weiser, *Handbook of Christian Feasts and Customs*, 65-66.
46.   Delumeau, *Catholicism Between Luther and Voltaire*, 169-197.
47.   Ibid., 177.
48.   Rupert Sheldrake, *The Rebirth of Nature: The Greening of Science and God* (Park Street Press, Rochester, Vermont, 1991) 40.
49.   Ibid., 43.
50.   Weiser, *Handbook of Christian Feasts and Customs*, 35.
51.   Delumeau, *Catholicism Between Luther and Voltaire*, 228.
52.   Ibid., 206.
53.   Thomas, *Religion and the Decline of Magic*, 151.
54.   Boorstin, *The Discoverers*, 571.
55.   Ibid., 571.
56.   Thomas, *Religion and the Decline of Magic*, 619-622.
57.   Ibid., 621.
58.   Ibid., 623.
59.   James 1:15.
60.   Thomas, *Religion and the Decline of Magic*, 38-39.
61.   2 Corinthians 5:6.
62.   Romans 8:13.
63.   Romans 8:6.
64.   Delumeau, *Sin and Fear*, 448.
65.   *The Merriam-Webster Dictionary* (New York: Pocket Books, 1974) 118.
66.   Saint Augustine, *The City of God* translated by Marcus Dods (New York: The Modern Library, 1950) Book 13, Ch.3, 413.
67.   Ibid., Book 13, Ch. 15, 423.

68. 1 Corinthians 15:26.
69. J.H. Strawley, *The Epistles of St. Ignatius, Bishop of Antioch* (London: Society for Promoting Christian Knowledge, 1900) 92-93.
70. Luke 20:34-36. (Underline added)
71. Delumeau, *Sin and Fear*, 54.
72. Ibid., 54.
73. John Bossy, *Christianity in the West 1400-1700* (Oxford: Oxford University Press, 1985) 26.
74. Thomas, *Religion and the Decline of Magic*, 603-604.
75. Ibid., 66.
76. Delumeau, *Sin and Fear*, 39.
77. Gaer and Siegel, *The Puritan Heritage: America's Roots in the Bible*, 92.
78. Augustine, *The City of God*, Book 13, Ch. 10, 419.
79. Ibid., Book 13, Ch. 4, 415.
80. Ecclesiastes 7:1.
81. Weiser, *Handbook of Christian Feasts and Customs*, 277.
82. Augustine, *The City of God*, Book 13, Ch. 4, 415.
83. Delumeau, *Sin and Fear*, 55.
84. Ibid., 352.
85. Matthew 16:28.
86. Thomas, *Religion and the Decline of Magic*, 142.

Chapter Ten - A World Without God

1. Shakespeare, *All's Well that Ends Well*, Act II, Scene iii.
2. Gary Zukav, *The Dancing Wu Li Masters* (Toronto: Bantam Books, 1979) 21-25.
3. Charles Darwin, *The Descent of Man and Selection in Relation to Sex* Part One, Volume III (New York, P.F. Collier & Son, 1871) 642.
4. Charles Darwin, *The Origin of Species by Means of Natural Selection or the Preservation of Favored Races in the Struggle for Life* Volume II (New York: D. Appleton & Co., 1897) 303.
5. Ibid., 294.
6. Jean Delumeau, *Catholicism Between Luther and Voltaire* (London: Burns and Oats, 1977) 204.
7. Frank Swancara, *Obstruction of Justice By Religion* (Denver: W. H. Courtwright Publishing Co., 1936) 27.
8. Frank E. Mauel, *The Changing of the Gods* (Hanover, NH: University Press of New England, 1983) 66.
9. John Locke, "A Letter Concerning Toleration," 1689 as printed in *The Founders' Constitution*, Volume 5 (Chicago: University of Chicago, 1987) 69.
10. Zukav, *The Dancing Wu Li Masters*, 26.
11. Fritjof Capra, *The Tao of Physics* (Toronto: Bantam Books, 1984) 8.
12. Stephen W. Hawking, *A Brief History of Time* (Toronto: Bantam Books, 1988) 55.

13.   Zukav, *The Dancing Wu Li Masters*, 27.
14.   Ibid., 38.
15.   Ibid., 80-83.
16.   Ibid., 82.
17   Ibid., 63.
18.   "Gaia: the Veiled Goddess", *The Economist*, December 22, 1990.
19.   Zukav, *The Dancing Wu Li Masters*, 29.
20.   Ibid., 297
21.   Andrew Kimbrell, "Body wars", *Utne Reader* (May/June 1992) 59.
22.   Joseph Gaer and Ben Siegel, *The Puritan Heritage: America's Roots in the Bible* (New York: Mentor Books, 1964) 29.
23.   Ibid., 77.
24.   Ibid., 78.
25.   *Treaties and Other International Acts of the United States of America*, edited by Hunter Miller, Volume 2 (Washington: United States Government Printing Office, 1931) 349-385, and Peter McWilliams, *Aint Nobody's Business If You Do: The Absurdity of Consensual Crimes in a Free Society* (Los Angeles: Prelude Press, 1993) 153.
26.   Ibid., 103-104.
27.   Ibid., 102.
28.   See note #25.
29.   Lawrence Lader, *Politics, Power & the Church* (New York: Macmillan Publishing Company, 1987) 135-140, "World Watch" *The Rocky Mountain News*, April 14, 1992, and "Vatican denies helping Nazis flee after war", The Associated Press, February 15, 1992.
30.   John Dollison, *Pope-Pourri* (New York: Simon & Schuster, 1994) 9.

Chapter Eleven - Conclusion

1.   Forrest G. Wood, *The Arrogance of Faith* (New York: Alfred A. Knopf, 1990) 27.

Selected Bibliography

Ackerman, Robert W. *Backgrounds to Medieval English Literature.* New York: Random House, 1966.

Achterberg, Jeanne. *Woman As Healer.* Boston: Shambala, 1991.

Adler, Margot Adler *Drawing Down the Moon.* New York: Beacon Press, 1979.

Anderson, William. *Green Man.* London and San Francisco: Harpercollins, 1990.

Ankarloo, Bengt and Henningsen, Gustav. *Early Modern European Witchcraft Centres and Peripheries.* Oxford: Clarendon Press, 1990.

Aquinas, Saint Thomas. *Summa Theologica.* New York & London: Blackfriars, McGraw-Hill, Eyre & Spottiswoode.

Armstrong, Karen. *Holy War: The Crusades and Their Impact on Today's World.* New York: Doubleday, 1988.

——————. *The Gospel According to Woman: Christianity's Creation of the Sex War in the West.* New York: Doubleday, 1986.

Ashe, Geoffrey. *The Virgin: Mary's Cult and the Re-emergence of the Goddess.* London: Arkana, 1976, 1988.

Augustine, Saint. *The City of God,* Book XIV, Ch.4, translated by Marcus Dods. New York: The Modern Library, 1950.

Baigent, Michael; Leigh, Richard; Lincoln, Henry, *Holy Blood, Holy Grail* New York: Dell, 1982.

Baroja, Julio Caro. *The World of Witches.* Chicago: University of Chicago Press, 1961.

Begg, Ian. *The Cult of the Black Virgin.* London: Arkana, 1985.

Boorstin, Daniel J. *The Discoverers.* New York: Random House, 1983.

Bossy, John. *Christianity in the West 1400-1700.* Oxford: Oxford University Press, 1985.

Burckhardt, Jacob. *The Civilization of the Renaissance in Italy.* edited by Irene Gordon. New York: Mentor Books, 1960.

Capra, Fritjof. *The Tao of Physics.* Toronto: Bantam Books, 1984.

Carmichael, Joel. *The Birth of Christianity.* New York: Hippocrene Books, 1989.

Cotterell, Arthur. *Myths and Legends.* New York: MacMillan Publishing Company, 1989.

Coulton, G.G. *Inquisition and Liberty*. Glouster, MA: Peter Smith, 1969.

Daniel-Rops, H. *Cathedral and Crusade*. New York: E.P.Dutton & Company, Inc., 1957.

Darwin, Charles. *The Descent of Man and Selection in Relation to Sex*. Part One, Volume III. New York, P.F. Collier & Son, 1871.

——————, *The Origin of Species by Means of Natural Selection or the Preservation of Favored Races in the Struggle for Life* Volume II. New York: D. Appleton & Co., 1897.

Delumeau, Jean. *Catholicism Between Luther and Voltaire*. London: Burns and Oats, 1977.

——————. *Sin and Fear*, translated by Eric Nicholson. New York: St. Martins Press, 1990.

Dollison, John. *Pope-Pourri*. New York: Simon & Schuster, 1994.

Edwards, Jonathan. "The Justice of God in the Damnation of Sinners," from *The Works of Jonathan Edwards, A.M.* London: Henry G. Bohn.

Eisler, Riane. *The Chalice and the Blade*. San Francisco: Harper & Row, 1987.

Essene Gospel of Peace, The. edited and translated by Edmond Bordeaux Szekely. San Diego: Academy of Creative Living, 1971.

Excerpta Ex Theodoto of Clement of Alexandria, The. translated by Robert Pierce Casey. London: Christophers, 1934.

Frazer, Sir James George. *The Golden Bough*. Vol.1 abridged edition. New York: Collier Books, 1922.

Ferguson, Evrett; McHugh, Michael P.; Norris, Frederick W. *Encyclopedia of Early Christianity*. New York & London: Garland Publishing, 1990.

Gaer,Joseph and Siegel, Ben. *The Puritan Heritage: America's Roots in the Bible*. New York: Mentor Books, 1964.

Graham, Lloyd M. *Deceptions and Myths of the Bible*. New York: Citadel Press, 1975.

Haskins, Charles Homer. *The Renaissance of the 12th Century*. Cleveland & New York: Meridian Books, 1927.

Haught, James A. *Holy Horrors*. Buffalo: Prometheus, 1990.

Hawking, Stephen W. *A Brief History of Time*. Toronto: Bantam Books, 1988.

Heer, Friedrich. *The Medieval World*. translated by Janet Sondheimer, New York: NAL, 1961.

Hillgarth, J.N. *The Conversion of Western Europe*. Englewood Cliffs, NJ: Prentice Hall, 1969.

Hippolytus Philosophumena 6.9, Volume II, Translated by F. Legge. London: Society For Promoting Christian Knowledge, 1921.

Howe Jr., Quincy. *Reincarnation For The Christian*. Philadelphia: Westminster Press, 1974.

Ignatius. *Magnesians* and *Trallians*. In the *Ante-Nicene Christian Library*. Edinburgh: T&T Clark.

Irenaeus. *Irenaeus Against Heresies*. In the *Ante-Nicene Christian Library*. Edinburgh: T&T Clark.

Irenaeus. *Irenaeus Against Heresies*. In the *Ante- Nicene Christian Library*. Buffalo: The Christian Literature Publishing Co., 1885.

Kamen, Henry. *Inquisition and Society in Spain*. Bloomington: Indiana University Press, 1985.

Karlsen, Carol F. *The Devil in the Shape of a Woman*. Vintage Books: New York, 1987.

Kimbrell, Andrew. "Body wars", *Utne Reader* (May/June 1992).

Kimsey, John. "The Code of Love," *GNOSIS*, No.18 (Winter 1991).

Kramer, Heinrich and James Sprenger, *The Malleus Maleficarum*. Translated by Montague Summers. New York: Dover Publications, 1971.

Lader, Lawrence. *Politics, Power & the Church*. New York: Macmillan Publishing Company, 1987.

Lea, Henry C. *History of Sacerdotal Celibacy in the Christian Church*. 4th edition revised. London: Watts & Co., 1932.

———————. *The Inquisition of the Middle Ages*. Abridgement by Margaret Nicholson. New York: MacMillan, 1961.

Levack, Brian P. *The Witch-Hunt in Early Modern Europe*. London: Longman, 1987.

Locke, John. "A Letter Concerning Toleration," 1689 as printed in *The Founders' Constitution*, Volume 5. Chicago: University of Chicago, 1987.

Lopez, Barry Holstun. *Of Wolves and Men*. New York: Charles Scribner's Sons, 1978.

Margolis, Jon. "War of words over Columbus rages on" *The Sunday Denver Post*, July 28, 1991.

Martin, Malachi. *Decline and Fall of the Roman Church*. New York: G.P. Putnam's Sons, 1981.

Mauel, Frank E. *The Changing of the Gods*. Hanover, NH: University Press of New England, 1983.

McWilliams, Peter. *Aint Nobody's Business If You Do: The Absurdity of Consensual Crimes in a Free Society*. Los Angeles: Prelude Press, 1993.

Mulligan, Hugh A. "Columbus Saga Sinking Fast" Associated Press, March 8, 1992.

Nag Hammadi Library, The. James M. Robinson, Director. New York: Harper & Row, 1977.

New Columbia Encyclopedia, The. edited by William H. Harris and Judith S. Levey (New York & London: Columbia University Press, 1975.

Nigg, Walter. *The Heretics: Heresy Through the Ages*. Edited and translated by Richard and Clara Winston. New York: Dorset Press, 1962.

Noonan, Jr., John T. *Contraception*. New York and Toronto: The New American Library, 1965.

Nottingham, Theodore. "The Birth Within: Meister Eckhart and the Knowing of God" *GNOSIS*, No.18 (Winter 1991).

O'Grady, Joan. *The Prince of Darkness*. Longmead: Element Books, 1989.

O'Neill, Timothy. "Century of Marvels, Century of Light" 14-18 and Judith Mann. "The Legend of the Cathars" *GNOSIS*, No.4.

Pagels, Elaine. *Adam, Eve and the Serpent*. New York: Random House, 1988.

—————. *The Gnostic Gospels*. New York: Random House, 1979.

Panati, Charles. *Panati's Extraordinary Endings of Practically Everything*. New York: Harper & Row, 1989.

Panati, Charles. *Extraordinary Origins of Everyday Things*. New York: Harper & Row, 1987.

Plaidy, Jean. *The Spanish Inquisition*. New York: Citadel Press, 1967.

Regenstein, Lewis. *Replenish the Earth*. New York: Crossroad, 1991.

Robbins, Rossell Hope. *The Encyclopedia of Witchcraft and Demonology*. New York: Bonanza Books, 1981.

Roth, Cecil. *The Spanish Inquisition*. New York: W. W. Norton & Company, 1964.

Russell, Jeffrey Burton. *A History of Medieval Christianity*. New York: Thomas Y. Cromwell, 1968.

—————. *Witchcraft in the Middle Ages*. Ithaca & London: Cornell University Press, 1972.

Schaff, Phillip. *History of the Christian Church*. Vol. V: The Middle Ages Grand Rapids, MI: Wm. B. Eerdmans, 1952.

Secret Teachings of Jesus, The. translated by Marvin W. Meyer. New York: Random House, 1984.

Shannon, Albert Clement. *The Medieval Inquisition*. Washington D.C.: Augustinian College Press, 1983.

Sheldrake, Rupert Sheldrake. *The Rebirth of Nature: The Greening of Science and God*. Park Street Press, Rochester, Vermont, 1991.

Smith, Charles Merrill. *The Pearly Gates Syndicate*. New York: Doubleday, 1971.

Smith, Joan. *Misogynies: Reflections on Myths and Malice*. New York: Fawcett Columbine, 1989.

Smith, John Holland. *The Death of Classical Paganism*, New York: Charles Scribner, 1976.

St. *Irenaeus, Proof of the Apostolic Preaching*. translated and annotated by Josephy P. Smith. Westminster, Maryland: The Newman Press, 1952.

Starr, Tama. *The "Natural Inferiority" of Women*. New York: Poseidon Press, 1991.

Stone, Merlin. *When God Was a Woman*. New York: Dorset Press, 1976.

Strawley, J.H. *The Epistles of St. Ignatius, Bishop of Antioch*. London: Society for Promoting Christian Knowledge, 1900.

Summers, Montague. *The History of Witchcraft and Demonology*. New York: New Hyde Park, 1956.

Swancara, Frank. *Obstruction of Justice By Religion*. Denver: W. H. Courtwright Publishing Co., 1936.

Tannahill, Reay. *Sex In History*. Michigan: Scarborough House, 1992.

Tertullian, "On Prescription Against Heretics" and "On the Flesh of Christ". *Ante-Nicene Fathers; Translations of the Writings of the Fathers down to A.A. 325*, Vol. III. Grand Rapids: Wm. B. Eerdmans Publishing Company, 1951.

Tertullian. *Tertullianus against Marcion*. In the *Ante-Nicene Christian Library*. Edinburgh: T&T Clark.

Thomas, Keith. *Religion and the Decline of Magic*. New York: Charles Scribner's Sons, 1974.

Tompkins, Peter. "Symbols of Heresy" in *The Magic of Obelisks*. New York: Harper, 1981.

Tuchman, Barbara W. *A Distant Mirror*. New York: Ballantine Books, 1978.

von Campenhausen, Hans. *Ecclesiastical Authority and Spiritual Power: In the Church of the First Three Centuries*, Translated by J.A. Baker. Stanford University Press, 1969.

Walker, Barbara G. *The Woman's Dictionary of Symbols and Sacred Objects* San Francisco: Harper & Row, 1988.

——————. *The Woman's Encyclopedia of Myths and Secrets*. San Francisco: Harper & Row, 1983.

Weiser, Francis X. *Handbook of Christian Feasts and Customs*. New York: Harcourt, Brace & Co., 1952.

Wood, Forrest. *The Arrogance of Faith*. New York: Alfred A. Knopf, 1990.

Zukav, Gary. *The Dancing Wu Li Masters*. Toronto: Bantam Books, 1979.

Index

Illustration Credits

Figure 2.1 Constantine I on horse. BETTMANN ARCHIVE. (SF1355) Figure 2.2 Trinity. LIBRARY OF CONGRESS. Figure 2.3 Crucifixion. LIBRARY OF CONGRESS. Figure 2.4 Virgin and Child. LIBRARY OF CONGRESS. Figure 3.1 Saint Augustine. LIBRARY OF CONGRESS. Figure 4.1 Chart of blood-letting points. LIBRARY OF CONGRESS. Figure 4.2 Book burning. LIBRARY OF CONGRESS. Figure 4.3 Saint Gregory the Great. LIBRARY OF CONGRESS. Figure 5.1 "Madonna as Protectress" NATIONAL GALLERY OF ART, Washington, Rosenwald Collection. Figure 5.2 "Madonna in a Wreath of Roses" NATIONAL GALLERY OF ART, Washington, Rosenwald Collection. Figure 5.3 Pope Urban Preaching the Crusades. SAN FRANCISCO PUBLIC LIBRARY. Figure 5.4 The Crusaders Enter Constaninople. LIBRARY OF CONGRESS. Figure 5.5 Pope Innocent III. LIBRARY OF CONGRESS. Figure 6.1 "Torture Chamber" SAN FRANCISCO PUBLIC LIBRARY. Figure 6.2 Auto-da-fé. LIBRARY OF CONGRESS. Figure 6.3 "First Landing of Columbus in the New World." LIBRARY OF CONGRESS. Figure 6.4 "The Execution of the Inca." LIBRARY OF CONGRESS. Figure 7.1 Martin Luther. LIBRARY OF CONGRESS. Figure 7.2 "Massacre of the Protestants in Calabria." LIBRARY OF CONGRESS. Figure 7.3 "The Massacre of St. Bartholomew." SAN FRANCISCO PUBLIC LIBRARY. Figure 7.4 John Knox. LIBRARY OF CONGRESS. Figure 7.5 "The Papal Gorgon, 1581, Reign of Elizabeth." SAN FRANCISCO PUBLIC LIBRARY. Figure 7.6 Demon by fire. LIBRARY OF CONGRESS. Figure 8.1 "Witches Sabbath" THE FINE ARTS MUSEUMS OF SAN FRANCISCO, Achenbach Foundation for Graphic Arts, Ludwig A. Emge, Ruth Haas Lilienthal Funds. Figure 8.2 Woman being tortured. LIBRARY OF CONGRESS. Figure 8.3 "The Witch No. 1" LIBRARY OF CONGRESS. Figure 8.4 Drawing of old woman. LIBRARY OF CONGRESS. Figure 8.5 Plantain. LIBRARY OF CONGRESS. Figure 9.1 "Pan" BETTMANN ARCHIVE. (PG10874) Figure 9.2 "Saint Alto" NATIONAL GALLERY OF ART, Washington, Rosenwald Collection. Figure 9.3 Martin Schongauer's painting of the annunciation, LIBRARY OF CONGRESS. Figure 9.4 "Fête Flamande" LIBRARY OF CONGRESS. Figure 9.5 Allegorical representation of time rewarding industry and punishing indolence. LIBRARY OF CONGRESS. **Figure 10.1** Camille Flammarion's "L'Atmosphere". LIBRARY OF CONGRESS **Figure 10.2** Isaac Newton. LIBRARY OF CONGRESS. **Figure 10.3** Charles Darwin. LIBRARY OF CONGRESS. **Figure 10.4** "Movement of human appendages and pulley systems compared using principles of mechanics and statics." 1680-1681. LIBRARY OF CONGRESS. **Figure 10.5** "The Aim of Pope Pius IX" LIBRARY OF CONGRESS.

About the Author

Helen Ellerbe was born in Beirut, Lebanon, grew up in Saudi Arabia, and was educated in Connecticut, Colorado and Germany. She has worked as a German translator, a Fortune 500 sales representative, a stockbroker, a sculptor of mythological figures, and most recently, as a researcher, writer, and public speaker. She lives in the San Francisco Bay Area with her husband.